Laura Dowling

FLORAL DIPLOMACY

AT THE WHITE HOUSE

Laura Dowling

FLORAL DIPLOMACY

AT THE WHITE HOUSE

stichting
kunstboek

This book is dedicated to
THE PURSUIT OF BEAUTY

and in memory of my father
Chief Warrant Officer Robert Moffett Dowling
U.S. Army

CONTENTS

FLOWERS AS A TOOL
FOR INNOVATION AND CHANGE

Flowers have a special place in our lives. Though transient and fleeting, flowers are important expressions and make lasting impressions. Flowers are part of all human ceremonies and life's turning points, including birthdays, anniversaries, weddings and funerals. They are also a mainstay in diplomatic relations, providing a visual and symbolic backdrop for meetings of heads of state, visiting dignitaries, and major events such as state dinners and G-8 summits.

Seven years ago, when the country was teetering on the edge of economic collapse and the new administration was focused on stabilizing the economy and preventing the downturn from becoming a depression, White House flowers were probably not at the top of policymakers' minds as a tool for innovation and optimism. Yet, an intriguing thing happened. The long-time White House florist retired after 30 years. Departing from the typical practice of hiring friends and family of existing residence staff for permanent White House positions, the Obama administration opened the application process for Chief Floral Designer to everyone. With an intuitive insight that flowers could be important symbolically and historically, First Lady Michelle Obama sponsored a talent-based competition to select a new florist based on a nation-wide search. She understood that flowers convey special meaning. By opening up the competition to all citizens, she underscored the point that in this country, what you achieve is based on what you do and not on who you know or where you come from. It was a powerful message consistent with a new spirit of optimism, hope and change.

At the time, I was a part-time florist working out of my basement kitchen. I had just provided floral arrangements for the opening of the new Chinese Embassy and thought I might be able to help the White House express its new style and strategic vision. I was inspired to enter this open competition and make a case that flowers can serve more than a decorative purpose – that they can convey and support nuanced policy goals. Multiple rounds of interviews culminated in an intense floral competition and interview with the First Lady. I was surprised and honored to be chosen to be the White House Chief Floral Designer. It proved that following a passion can lead to extraordinary things, and anything is possible in America with perseverance and a commitment to excellence.

During my initial interview with the First Lady, we discussed transforming the traditional White House floral program into a new platform for collaboration and innovation. We talked about using flowers to highlight inspirational messages regarding Administration programs, American traditions and environmental themes as well as introducing a fresh design aesthetic that would fit within the context of what is appropriate for the iconic White House setting. We opened up the flower shop to talented volunteers from across the country and sought opportunities for linking flower displays with key policy initiatives. By dramatically expanding the volunteer program, we increased design quality and capacity and overall efficiency.

The flower shop became a dynamic and creative place, highlighting the administration's goals and aspirations. When the U.S. winter Olympic team visited the White House, they carried a visual symbol of both the Olympic experience and the First Lady's "Let's Move" Initiative – an Olympic torch made out of green beans, artichokes and carrots. As they marched across the South Lawn with the vegetable torch held high, the athletes conveyed the essence of the signature program – an active lifestyle combined with healthy eating – that was incredibly effective. We innovated again, linking program initiatives with Memorial Day wreath-making. Typically, staff and contractors were hired to work on the holiday weekend to create seven red, white and blue Presidential wreaths for placement at war memorials, including the Tomb of the Unknown Soldier at Arlington Cemetery. In 2014, for the first time and in collaboration with the First Lady's "Joining Forces" initiative, we invited a dozen Gold Star military family members to volunteer their help in making the memorial wreaths. I saw firsthand the symbolic power of involving the people who experience the meaning of Memorial Day in a profoundly personal way.

To address another priority – science and technology – we pioneered a new partnership with the White House Office of Science and Technology Policy (OSTP) and the Presidential Innovation Fellows team. This was a special challenge – flowers and technology. To make our point, we collaborated on creating robotic versions of Bo and Sunny (the First Family dogs), 3-D printed ornaments, and an interactive 3-D digital snow-scape design, integrating new technologies with White House holiday décor and synchronizing policy themes such as innovation and technology with traditional holiday themes. While the technology we used for the "Bo-bots" was not complex, the nexus with custom design and artistic details allowed us to create something totally unexpected, and spawned additional ideas for linking technology and design.

Flowers at the White House have always highlighted traditions and added beauty to the period rooms. In the last few years, they have taken on an expanded strategic role. Flowers at the White House are truly power flowers. Whether they are in the Oval Office, Cabinet Room or Roosevelt Room or placed throughout the public tour route in the Executive Mansion, their value extends beyond decorative purposes to encompass a larger mission. *This is the concept of Floral Diplomacy.* It was my great honor and privilege to serve the President and First Lady as Chief Floral Designer at the White House and I am proud that together we created an inspiring spirit of innovation, collaboration and change.

MY STORY

ON THE FARM

Growing up in in the shadow of Mt. St. Helens and Mt. Rainier in the rolling farm country of the Pacific Northwest, I learned to appreciate the beauty of nature from a young age. Our farmhouse cottage in Chehalis, Washington, included a large and charming garden (created by a previous owner) with heirloom roses in every shade, a spring bulb garden, a variety of perennials, Japanese maples and a weeping willow tree. Each spring, hundreds of blooming fuchsia, pink and lavender rhododendron shrubs ringed our property on Newaukum Hill, painting the landscape in swaths of vibrant hues. There was a large vegetable patch, a fruit orchard with cherry, apple and pear trees, and a 20-acre field of native grasses and wildflowers where our horses, sheep and a pony roamed. It was a high-maintenance property that came with a long list of weekly chores, including a great deal of weeding and upkeep of the garden, led by my grandmother, the head gardener. I especially loved the fruit orchard – this is where the changing seasons were most obvious and the beauty of the landscape was on full and dramatic display. In the gray and soggy winter months, pale green lichen moss covered all of the barren tree branches, giving the orchard a beautiful, yet somewhat eerie, ghostly appearance. By spring, the orchard exploded into colorful, fragrant blossoms that danced and swayed in the breeze, the petals eventually falling and covering the field in a sea of pink and white blooms. My favorite iteration of the orchard landscape was always the height of summer into the early fall when the branches were so heavily laden with fruit that they would almost touch the ground. My siblings and I would harvest the ripe cherries, pears and apples to enjoy all season long in home-made pies, preserves and seasonal crafting projects – if they didn't become "friendly fire" ammunition hurled by my brother first!

Not too far away from the gentle pastures of our family farm, the rugged terrain of the Cascade Mountains rises from verdant lowlands, beckoning outdoorsmen, hikers and campers alike with its unparalleled, breathtaking beauty. My family and I often went on summer camping excursions deep into the remote Goat Rock Wilderness preserve, occasionally on the hunt for wild blackberries and huckleberries that my grandmother would turn into tasty cobblers and winter preserves. For many years, we spent summers at my great-grandparents' rustic beach cabin near Priest Point Park where we hiked down a narrow path to reach this remote, yet spectacular retreat situated high on cliffs above Puget Sound. Here, we would go on nature hikes, enjoy clambakes on the beach, and roast marshmallows around campfires under the starry summer skies. I can still remember the smell of rain and cedar, evergreen forests, and the pungent low-tide air. In this pristine setting of fir trees, mist and fog where the lush green vegetation stood out in vivid contrast to the intense blue summer skies – which were inevitably obscured by low-hanging gray clouds in winter – the colors of flowers took on an exaggerated effect. Here, fuschia and violet rhododendron blooms, the size of platters, flourished, along with pink and blue hydrangea and meadow wildflowers in every shade. Set against a background of mosses, foliage and trees in every shade of green, brown and gray, the floral profusion glowed in glorious technicolor displays. I have no doubt that growing up in such close proximity to the landscape, surrounded by the epic splendor of the Pacific Northwest, gave me a lifelong appreciation of nature, a sensitivity to composition and colors, flowers and the aspiration to create beauty.

Against this romantic backdrop of my rural northwest heritage, I was motivated to explore the world beyond my small-town country life. Because it was the 1980s and exciting new frontiers of professional opportunity were open to women, I pursued a practical academic path, studying politics and policy at Centralia College and then transferring to the University of Washington in Seattle – the state's largest city. In college I joined the tennis and track teams, running middle distance races before moving up to marathon training and road racing. Armed with degrees in Political Science and Public Administration, I went to Washington D.C. on a graduate fellowship and launched a 25-year career in government relations and strategic communications. In the early 1990s, at the height of the dot.com boom, I even studied computer programming and networking, adding what was then an *au courant* feather to my professional cap. My academic and professional backgrounds taught me discipline, writing, problem-solving and analytical skills, as well as practical management principles and political savvy. My sports background demonstrated the value of teamwork and collaboration as well as the power of perseverance. In hindsight, it was the perfect training and experience for my eventual White House work.

PARIS INSPIRATION

My husband and I went to Paris for the first time in 2000. It made a huge impression on me. From the moment I landed in the City of Light, I was in awe of the art and architecture, parks and bistros, French cuisine, couture fashion and, of course, the flowers. My first impression was that Paris has an effervescent quality as if everywhere I looked there was an element of extreme exuberance: the Eiffel Tower's twinkly lights that illuminate the night sky; the bronze horses atop the Grand Palais that seem to leap and gallop in mid-air; the stone carvings at the Louvre that are as detailed and delicate as if they had been carved in icing; the flowering plants in the Jardin des Tuileries that appear to be dancing in the sun. Paris exudes a sense of lightness, beauty and artistic achievement that for me is exemplified and distilled in the French bouquet.

We toured the city on foot, exploring many of the sights – both famous and hidden – that Paris has to offer. As we walked around the 6th arrondissement of St. Germain de Pres, the beautiful and historic neighborhood on Paris' Left Bank, we stumbled upon the flower boutique of renowned Parisian florist Christian Tortu. The bouquet of sweet peas, rose hips and lady's mantle in the window was arranged in such a compelling composition that it literally stopped me in my tracks. There was something so moving about the level of artistry in that little bouquet. It was poignant, poetic and romantic, and underscored the ethereal nature of flowers and life. Upon reflection, I also noticed that it had a sense of vitality and joyful abandon that was echoed in the Parisian cityscape and gardens. I was drawn to the poetry and artistry of Tortu's beautiful compositions. They were lively and expressive, exuding beauty. I was struck by the power and emotion emanating from these artistic floral creations.

CHATEAU DE CHENONCEAU

On that same trip, we visited the famous French chateaus of the Loire Valley, including the Château de Chenonceau, a romantic 16th century castle that spans the Cher River. With its blend of late Gothic and early Renaissance architecture, notable collections of antique furnishings and decorative arts and lovely gardens, the chateau is full of beauty and inspiration. While the Flemish tapestries, carved oak furniture and landscape paintings were impressive, the flowers by far stole the show. In every room, charming displays of fresh flowers from the gardens brought color and a sense of liveliness to the grand spaces, making the rooms seem more intimate and welcoming. In the entry hall, a giant wheat-covered basket of all-white lilies was displayed on a 16th century table – the bouquet was stunning in its elegant simplicity. The main parlor featured two large classical iron urns filled with topiaries made entirely of colorful vegetables and gourds. The arrangements were unexpected, as well as quite beautiful. In another room, a fireplace mantel decorated with cherry topiaries wrapped in small pots of fresh rosemary set the perfect tone – natural, elegant and classic – yet conveying a decidedly fresh and modern vibe. It was incredible to see how the flowers (and fruits and vegetables) could totally transform the character and feeling of this imposing space. I especially noticed how the beautiful organic containers of leaves, wheat and herbs, combined with the fresh flower arrangements just picked from the garden created a jaunty insouciance – a look of casual elegance that was both striking and appropriate in the opulently decorated historic rooms.

So in that moment of inspiration, I decided to become a florist, challenging myself to see if I could capture the power and emotion of flowers. As a result of that trip, I was so inspired that I felt compelled to explore French floral design as a unique art form. When I returned home I tried to re-create this style of flower arranging that I found so inspiring. I quickly realized that it was not so simple, that it was much more difficult than it looked. The art of floral design at the level I saw in Paris and the Loire Valley involved specific techniques and a clear design philosophy. I was determined to learn.

L'ECOLE DES FLEURS

A friend told me about a new flower school at the Crillon Hotel in Paris, L'Ecole des Fleurs, that was coincidentally headed by Christian Tortu. I signed up for classes and went back to Paris. While I worked a full-time job at The Nature Conservancy, the world's largest conservation agency, I travelled to Paris once or twice a year on vacation to study flowers. At the same time, I started a part-time floral design business, working out of my home studio (my basement kitchen) focusing on French flower design. I created a website and started a blog, working nights and weekends on flowers, while still working full-time at my day job. Most nights I stayed up past 2 a.m., studying flowers, perfecting techniques, creating bouquets for clients to be delivered the next day. I loved working with flowers so much that the challenge of juggling schedules and obligations with the opportunity to pursue my passion was energizing and motivating rather than draining. At the time, I wasn't sure where my budding flower career would lead me; my focus was simply on following my passion and becoming an expert in the field.

MY FLORAL STUDIO

While I was a part-time florist operating out of my home studio near Washington, D.C., I held a full-time job while pursuing my floristry career in the evenings and on weekends. It was the perfect set-up for dabbling in, observing and participating in the world of "official floristry" in the nation's capital. As I embarked upon my floral career, I remember one evening in particular that made a big impression on me. I was invited to attend a fancy event at the National Gallery of Art. It was a special evening honoring private donors, a preview party for a major exhibit. I was especially excited to see the flowers, which I knew would be spectacular. We entered the grand space that was decorated with lavish displays of opulent flowers, tall vases stuffed full of roses, lilies and orchids, room after room of floral decorations. What was striking to me – and also disappointing – was the total lack of impact these arrangements had on the crowd. Throughout the evening, I watched people walk by the flowers, oblivious to the monumental expense and vast amount of flowers that went into these floral displays, paying no attention whatsoever to the intrinsic beauty of the flowers. The reaction was the polar opposite of what I had experienced in Paris where the flowers were so compelling.

What was the difference? It was fairly obvious. The flowers were created as boring rote designs, multiple copies of a single simplistic prototype. They appeared to have been made in a hurry, a half-hearted effort without artistry or soul, just uninspired design by committee. Any passion or feeling about the artistry of the design (and the venerable location) had long since dissipated by the time the bouquets were delivered to the National Gallery. The flowers were stiff and formulaic in a radial style, the most basic of all floral techniques. The lack of energy and listlessness in the designs were palpable, so no wonder people ignored them. They were the proverbial potted plants; forgotten wallflowers forlornly languishing in the room.

I realized that what attracted me to the French approach was the energy that the flowers exuded – a feeling of lightness and liveliness that created a spirit of joy and commanded attention. To me, this was exactly what floral arrangements should do – capture the beauty of nature: the colors, textures, movement and materials – and then re-interpret it creatively to complement interior décor. Flowers should create excitement and energy, lifting the spirits of people in the room. After several years of studying flowers in Paris, I finally discovered the technique for creating this feeling: a bouquet built in levels with an initial base structure of swirling greens (to create a sense of movement), followed by layers of overlapping greens and flowers with trailing vines and dancing branches. The structured bouquet with movement and lightness, made artistically rather than from a recipe, was the key to this approach.

My flower portfolio included creating flowers for a wide variety of private clients, embassies, galas and government officials, including former Vice President Cheney's residence at the Naval Observatory. I learned how to use flowers to express sentiments and emotions, design and implement large-scale projects, and to conceptualize flowers for official events. It was a perfect training ground for experimenting with flowers as a diplomatic and strategic tool, a precursor of floral diplomacy. Here are some of my memorable events:

The yellow bouquet of friendship. A florist is often called in to help out in life's difficult times. One time, a client called me with a special request: "I want to send a bouquet to my best friend who has just completed her third grueling round of chemotherapy. She described the heartfelt sentiment she wanted to convey to her friend via flowers. "I want this to be the most beautiful bouquet she has ever seen in her life. When she receives the flowers, I want her to feel happy that she's alive." I said that I would do my very best. It was early spring in D.C. and the delicate spring flowers were in full bloom: daffodils, narcissus, tulips and flowering branches. My idea was to create a bouquet that evoked the symbolism of spring, the rebirth of the earth, and the essence of life itself – with flowers arranged as if they were bursting forth from the barren ground, defying winter's grasp. I wanted to capture that magical moment when life and light appear after the depths of winter darkness. Shortly after I delivered the flowers, I received a beautiful note from the woman. She said that the bouquet made her both smile and weep – it was an acknowledgement of the suffering she had endured, the symbolism of the hope and promise of spring – and what she saw as the miracle of her recovery. The flowers symbolized the indomitable spirit of life and the solidarity and support of her special friend. I felt humbled by the experience and the power of flowers to transmit this nuanced message. In this case, floral diplomacy meant creating flowers that evoked feelings that words alone could not express.

Vivaldi's Four Seasons bouquets. One year I created designs that highlighted the connection between music and flowers. The theme for the annual American Horticultural Society's gala at historic River Farm in Alexandria, Virginia was "Music in the Garden" with world-renowned cellist Yo Yo Ma serving as the honorary chairman of the event. In a spectacular outdoor setting overlooking the Potomac River, surrounded by lush gardens in full bloom, my task was to create four large bouquets that conjured each season and the corresponding movements of Vivaldi's iconic piece. For this assignment, I drew on my musical background (12 years of piano study) and an understanding of the connection between the color wheel and the musical scale to create floral designs that evoked both music and nature. As the string quartet played Vivaldi that evening and the guests strolled through the beautiful gardens in peak bloom, the Four Seasons bouquets created a visual focal point, a way of connecting music, flowers, and gardens to engage all of the senses, amplifying the experience.

Bouquets of a 1,000 Roses. As a symbol of tribute, flowers make a memorable statement, honoring a person's life through beauty and symbolism – and sometimes through sheer volume and impact. In 2006, the Embassy of Haiti commissioned me to create two giant bouquets of 1,000 roses as a tribute to Katherine Dunham, the famous American choreographer, for a festival of "Yanvalou" performed at the John F. Kennedy Center for the Performing Arts. Yanvalou is a Haitian celebration of spirits featuring a program of dance, drums and testimonials. Ms. Dunham spent years in Haiti, teaching dance and promoting philanthropic pursuits, becoming a beloved honorary citizen of the island nation. The rose was her favorite flower. In her honor, I created leaf-covered stands using the largest planter tubs I could find, hot-gluing thousands of individual leaves to the surface, representing the thousands of lives Ms. Dunham affected through her work in Haiti. I then filled these vessels with masses of roses. The big challenge of designing bouquets of 1,000 roses in my kitchen – beyond the stripping and processing of 2,000 individual stems – was the monumental task of delivering the 300 pound pieces to center stage at the Kennedy Center. With the assistance of four unsuspecting roofers in the neighborhood (who my husband commandeered) to help lift the heavy bouquets and a friend's borrowed refrigerated pastry truck to transport them, we delivered the bouquets to their center stage position. We were lucky to attend the performance that night, a magical and unforgettable display of music and dance as well as Haitian culture and tradition. Fortunately for us, the Haitian Embassy had plans for the flowers after the event so we were able to leave the massive arrangements behind. Like many things in life, I learned that floral diplomacy often comes down to simple logistics.

Historic traditions. For several years, I served on a design committee that promotes the Historic Alexandria Foundation, a non-profit group that protects the historic buildings and neighborhoods of Alexandria, Virginia. Each year, we explored different historical themes such as the art of the bouquet, the art of dining, life's little luxuries, living with antiques and other topics. The goal was to highlight historical themes that connect us to our past through a series of photojournalistic essays. Through this position, I gained valuable experience working with historic collections, beautiful antiques, and creating floral designs that balanced and enhanced period rooms. I saw that floral diplomacy requires an understanding of history, tradition and interior design to bridge the gap between past and present and fully integrate flowers with historic spaces.

Environmental themes. Before my White House position, I often created floral arrangements that carried out environmental themes. My previous employer, The Nature Conservancy, occasionally commissioned me to iterate key messages related to their conservation mission. One year I created animal topiaries for a Board of Directors' event where each centerpiece design highlighted a species in its native habitat. Another time, when the Conservancy hosted First Lady Laura Bush at an elegant luncheon, I designed flowers that represented landscapes across the country, including a Texas hill country display for her table. The décor I provided at the Conservancy's international conferences typically featured locally grown flowers (with a low carbon footprint), re-usable and recyclable containers, and a labor model that involved partnering with local garden clubs to create the floral designs. In this case, where the flowers were grown, the materials we used, and how we worked – all became part of the story of linking flowers as a decorative element with strategic objectives.

Chinese embassy. On a couple of memorable occasions, my floral studio work took on an air of international mystery and intrigue. When I was commissioned by the Chinese Embassy to create large, statement pieces for the grand opening of their I.M. Pei-designed building in Washington, D.C., it involved multiple intense meetings and site visits with Chinese officials over a period of several weeks to understand the special nature and scope of this assignment. I quickly realized that flowers were very important in Chinese culture and would be a key symbolic feature of this historic event. I took pages of notes during the meetings about the colors and types of flowers that could be used (red flowers, carnations, anthuriums) and those I had to avoid (white flowers, red roses – which were deemed "too romantic"), as well as detailed style and size requirements. I was fascinated by the discussion of flowers as a symbolic, diplomatic and cultural tool – a key element for setting the tone of the ceremony. One centerpiece had to fit an enormous 16 ft. round table that seats 32 people. I used a child's wading pool as the container for this arrangement. Another large bouquet was designated for a room that featured amazing works of Chinese art, including a priceless antique screen with a galloping horse motif. This arrangement had to be over 10 ft. tall to make a statement in the cavernous room. For this container, I stacked two of the largest planter containers I could find end on end, covering them in leaves to create a giant organic, yet classic hourglass vase. In addition, I created a dozen smaller arrangements to decorate the "meeting rooms" – large square rooms that featured beautiful Chinse art and comfortable chairs and side tables that lined the walls. I designed the two large arrangements in my kitchen – which was akin to building ships in a bottle – and somehow managed to get them to the Embassy where a dozen Chinese men hand-carried them to the security building and then into the rooms where they were displayed.

The organizers invited my husband and me to stay for the reception, which was attended by over 900 people. A journalist from the China Press Newspaper approached me for an impromptu interview about my flowers and role in the grand opening event. The article was published on the front page, and went into extensive details about my flowers. I was struck by the level of interest in the grand opening flowers and their symbolism that made my work a front page story – (even if some of our quotes were lost in translation).

A few months later, the Chinese Embassy called me again. "Are you available for a flower project,?" my Embassy handler asked. "Yes, what is the date?" I responded. "When are you available?" came his cryptic and vague reply. "Well, this weekend could work," I said, "Saturday or Sunday." "Sunday is best," he confirmed. He gave me the details for the project – another large centerpiece for the 16 ft. table and a few smaller bouquets, along with the color requirements: the designs must use flowers in all shades of red. And there were specific security requirements, too – he told me to avoid using any wire or tubes in the flower arrangements – and, in a very unusual twist, he said that he would come to my studio (in my kitchen) to watch me create the pieces and ride in with us to deliver the pieces to the Chinese Embassy. He did not reveal the purpose of the event, which seemed to be shrouded in secrecy, but said I would be "very happy" when I found out about it afterwards. I was very intrigued by the mystery and unusual logistical arrangements surrounding this project.

So I bought another wading pool and created a large centerpiece with 7 smaller satellite bouquets that would surround the piece. In Chinese culture, the sun with 7 orbiting moons is a symbolic motif. The concept conveyed special meaning – and served a practical purpose as well. The table was so large that it required additional elements to create an aesthetically balanced display. My Chinese Embassy friend ended up spending a whole day with me as I prepared all of the flowers in my kitchen.

When we arrived at the Embassy, flowers in tow, there was a palpable air of excitement and energy. We put the flowers on a conveyor belt that went into a large security building, the flowers disappearing behind a black curtain at the opening, emerging a while later from another opening. Huge red banners with Chinese lettering draped the entrance of the Embassy. My handler smiled and said that he looked forward to telling me about the special mystery guest who would be arriving. He took pictures of me standing in front of the flowers once they were placed in the room. As promised, he called after the event and said that it was the President of China who visited the new Chinese Embassy where a special dinner was held in his honor. My flowers were the centerpiece for this official event.

U.S. ELECTION NIGHT, PARIS

My husband and I spent presidential election night November, 2008 in Paris, France as part of a week-long visit. I was studying French flower design with a Parisian master florist at her studio near the Louvre. As we sat in our hotel room watching the election coverage, we felt inspired to celebrate this historic election with fellow Americans. It turns out there were several exciting options for gathering with the American expatriate community in Paris. The American Embassy was sponsoring a formal election watch event. Another election-themed party was being held at a restaurant on the Champs-Élysées. But we elected to go to a classic and casual place, Harry's American Bar near the Paris Opera House and La Madeleine church. It turns out that many people had the same idea. As we approached the Avenue of the Opera and Harry's Bar, we heard the loud crowd before we arrived. Incredibly, thousands upon thousands of Parisians had assembled in the center of Paris to celebrate the possibility of electing America's first African American president. Everywhere we looked, as far as we could see, people were smiling, singing and shouting, waving French and American flags that created an undulating sea of red, white and blue. There was excitement in the air and a palpable sense of joy.

We moved through the crowd to work our way closer to the entrance to Harry's, the focal point of the immense throng. There was a special election night event going on with a red carpet and rope and stanchions. Somehow we found ourselves at the entrance facing a rather large doorman who was checking IDs. The French bouncer disappeared inside for a minute and then came back and waved us both in. We found ourselves at a party where the mood was absolutely electric. The place was packed.

Veuve Cliquot champagne was flowing and the waiters floated around serving hot dogs on silver trays to all of the revelers. Flat screen television monitors were positioned everywhere, beaming in election updates from all the American network analysts. We were six hours ahead of Eastern Time, so the polls were still open across the country. It was a fabulous party.

We soon found a seat and took in the festive and boisterous scene. At one point, a French news anchor came up to me and in a breathless voice said 'say something to the French people.' Taken a bit off guard, I smiled and looked into the camera, waving 'bonsoir!' It was an incredible, unforgettable evening in a place that had hosted many well-known Americans who had visited Paris in the past century – Ernest Hemingway, George Gershwin, Scott and Zelda Fitzgerald. As we stepped back out into the night air, the crowds had grown even larger. I'll never forget that spirit of positive energy, the collective feeling of euphoria and sense of possibility that was in the air that night.

We left that magical place with the feeling of being happy to be there in that moment and so proud to be Americans. On that historic election night far away from home, we saw the essential spirit of America – the land of hope and dreams – in action, and on full display. It was powerful, exhilarating and very moving. In the ensuing years, I also saw up close and firsthand what happens when an outsider's aspirational vision runs headlong into an entrenched bureaucracy. Hope and change are exceedingly difficult to make real. However, since that electrifying night, I've never stopped believing in the power of the human spirit to overcome obstacles and effectuate change.

THE AMERICAN DREAM

In March, 2009, my husband called me with the news that the long-time White House florist had retired after 32 years. 'You should apply for the job,' he said. At the time, I was working as a part-time florist out of my basement kitchen, creating flowers and décor for a range of clients in Washington, D.C., including the Chinese Embassy, while working a full-time job in another field.

It turns out that many people had the same idea. There was great speculation about the prospect of a new and exciting direction for White House flowers and décor. Many observers foresaw 'edgier' and 'modern' tastes from the new First Family, while others speculated that the Obamas would favor a more traditional and elegant approach. The White House was flooded with hundreds of inquiries about a position that had heretofore been out of reach for several decades. White House officials established a dedicated telephone line with information on how to apply for the job. Unbeknownst to me, my husband called the White House, obtained the pertinent contact information and put it in front of me. Initially, I could not move past the long-shot nature of this proposition. No one sends in an unsolicited job application and expects to hear back, especially if the job is at 1600 Pennsylvania Avenue. Moreover, these kinds of coveted positions are always reserved for friends, family members and/or insiders with special political ties. So I rejected his idea. He was persistent. In fact, he pestered me for over a month to put together a resume and cover letter and mail it in.

Who would think that you could send in a 'cold call' application for the White House Chief Floral designer and be a serious contender? But that is exactly what happened. In June, 2009, while I was sitting in an internet café in small village in Germany, where I was taking flower classes, I received an e-mail from the White House notifying me that I was one of 12 semi-finalists. I was stunned. My excitement gave way to a bit of a panic when I realized that I only had a few days to put together a formal application – a complete portfolio, a cover letter and resume. And there I was in a remote – albeit idyllic – German village halfway around the world with only sporadic access to the Internet.

I contacted my photographer in Washington, D.C., arranged to create a portfolio of my work, and managed to send an overnight package to the White House before the deadline. When I returned from Germany, I busied myself with projects, not expecting to hear anything back. But within a month I was called in for an interview at the White House.

In late July, I met with several White House officials in the historic Map Room, located on the ground floor of the White House. The Map Room was named for its use during World War II, when President Franklin Roosevelt used it as a situation room to study maps to track the war's progress (for such purposes it was later replaced by the West Wing Situation Room). At that point, there were seven semi-finalists. Each applicant was interviewed by the same group in the same setting. I was led into the interview with the Chief Usher, Social Secretary, Chief Executive Officer of the White House, Events Usher and Social Office staffer. As I took my seat in an 18th century Chippendale arm chair, facing the imposing panel seated around me, I noted that the mood seemed a bit tense and strained. No one was smiling and everyone was spread out in the room which made it difficult to acknowledge the individual panelists.

The interview.

The Chief Usher, a retired Navy admiral and the first African American to hold the position, kicked off the interview with a standard question: 'Tell me a little something about yourself that is not on your resume,' he drawled in his native New Orleans accent. I described my background as a marathon runner which has given me great physical stamina and a high level of determination and personal resolve. The Events Usher, an elfin man with an intense, formal demeanor belying his extracurricular interest in the flying trapeze, was hired as the wine steward during the Clinton Administration. He was now the assistant usher in charge of White House events. 'How comfortable are you in selecting linens?' he asked. 'My design background and event planning credentials are extensive,' I replied, 'I've studied design for many years. Colors, fabrics, linens, china and entertaining are my passion and forte.' He nodded, approvingly.

The glamorous, Harvard-educated Social Secretary alluded to management and personnel challenges in the flower shop and asked me about my management experience and business credentials. 'How do you feel about entering a very difficult environment?' she asked. I told her about my long career in government relations and communications in Washington, D.C., including my most recent job as Senior Manager of Strategic Communications at The Nature Conservancy, citing specific examples of project management and team-building experience, as well as describing strategic planning accomplishments. She scribbled down a few notes in response. Her assistant asked 'What inspires you?' That was easy: 'I'm inspired by nature, art, architecture, fashion, interior design, history, literature, everything really,' I said – 'and especially, French flower design.' The panel noted that there would be increased budgetary constraints on White House décor, including flowers. 'Do you have images of simpler, 'everyday' office-style designs that you can show us? I replied that I would follow up immediately after the interview and send them specific examples of budget-friendly designs.

After the meeting, the Admiral's assistant met me and escorted me to the door. The Admiral thanked me for coming in and indicated that there were many candidates yet to be interviewed. He said that he would keep in touch and let me know if I was selected for the next round. In response to the panel's request for additional images, I created a new portfolio of simple one-color, one-flower designs and e-mailed them to the Social Secretary. I also mailed individual, hand-written follow up notes to everyone who interviewed me. I still felt that I was quite a long shot for the position.

The final round.

In September, 2009, I was travelling with a French furnishings company on business in Chicago. Working in collaboration with their marketing team, I was giving a series of in-store lectures and demonstrations on French flower design around the country. While on this trip, I received a call from the Chief Usher informing me that I was one of three finalists who would be invited in for a final competition and presentation to the First Lady. 'Congratulations,' he said, 'you've made it to the final round.' He explained that the logistics of the competition would be communicated in a follow up e-mail from his assistant, but he gave me a brief overview of how the competition would work. Each of us would be given the same assignment to make several arrangements within a four-hour time frame. We would each be sequestered in a separate room. We would be able to order our own flowers and bring in our own containers – or use White House vessels if desired. We could come in the day before the competition for 2 hours to process our flowers and select the presidential china for our table presentations. The date of the competition was set for October 7.

Later in the week, I received additional details about the competition from the Ushers' Office, including the specific floral designs that we would each be asked to make. The first assignment was to create a complete state dinner tableau for the Obamas' first state dinner with India, scheduled for late November. This involved selecting linens, china, glassware, candles, flowers and vases – everything to create a complete state dinner table setting. The White House would provide a 5 ft. round table and eight chairs for the competition display; each finalist would develop a concept and create proposed décor for the event. The second floral challenge was to design a large centerpiece arrangement for the Blue Room. The Blue Room is a beautiful oval-shaped room located on the main floor in the center of the White House. The flowers here are among the most visible and prominent on the public tour route display. For this challenge, the White House provided a pale blue silk tablecloth that we would use to coordinate flower selections. The final part of the competition involved creating a flower arrangement for the Oval Office. The White House asked each of us to provide a list of flowers that we would need for the competition. Then they scheduled a separate two hour block of time for us to come in to the White House flower shop on October 6 (the day before the competition) to prepare and organize the flowers, select the presidential china for our state dinner table setting, as well as any other pieces we wanted to use from the White House collection (e.g., vermeil pieces, porcelain bowls, candlesticks, etc.) in our décor presentation.

I prepared for the competition as if I were getting ready for a major speaking event like the Philadelphia flower show or a sporting event like the Boston Marathon. The first step was to research each assignment and map out a flower strategy and game plan. To get oriented, I read books on White House entertaining and décor and researched the rooms where I knew the competition pieces would be placed. I created a schedule and timeline for preparing containers, ordering flowers, as well as a work plan for the actual competition. I read President Obama's book 'The Audacity of Hope' to familiarize myself with his vision for the country. In addition, I developed a special flower brochure/treatise that illustrated my design philosophy and ideas for the White House flower program. Since I knew that I would not have much time with the First Lady during the interview, I wanted to be sure that my proposed new approach to flowers was strongly conveyed. With the help of a friend who worked in marketing, I created a little booklet that highlighted the strategies, concepts, colors, and container designs that the First Lady could read at her convenience..

A key part of my planning process included researching the customs & cultures of India. My inspiration for the state dinner color scheme was the Indian peacock, the national bird of India, a symbol of pride, beauty and grace. My idea was to create a beautiful table setting based on the peacock's purple, violet and apple green colors. I also looked at Oval Office photos and arrangements of flowers to get a sense of the colors and proportions of the space. For the Oval Office competition piece, I decided to create a seasonal display of copper and rust-colored roses with hydrangea and rosehips in an autumn-themed bouquet. This would set the appropriately beautiful, yet dignified and masculine tone.

For the final piece, the large Blue Room arrangement, I researched White House photos of the Blue Room that depicted flower arrangements over the years. The room ceiling is 18 feet tall, so the competition centerpiece had to be tall and substantial enough to fit the proportion of the room. In addition, it had to be created in the round, since it would be placed on the early 19th century marble-topped table in the middle of the room, visible from all sides. Most of the images of Blue Room flowers depicted all white, yellow or multi-color arrangements presented in porcelain bowls or vermeil urns. Given the vivid shade of cobalt blue décor in the room, I felt that it would be possible to explore a bold and modern palette of neighboring colors, including purple, lilac, blue and fuchsia in the floral displays. For my competition piece, I chose a selection of garden flowers in monochromatic shades of blue and lavender, including hydrangea, roses, delphinium and passion flower vine. As a new concept, I planned to introduce a hand-made organic container composed of alternating swirls of folded magnolia and lemon leaves, inspired by the wonderful designs I had seen in Paris. My goal was to demonstrate a clear example of the new garden style bouquet featuring an organic vessel covered in leaves and vines. This approach would best illustrate my idea for a natural, yet refined style that would be perfectly at home in this classic and iconic space.

The day before the competition, I went to the White House at my appointed time, around midday, to unpack and organize my flowers for the competition. A White House butler showed me the George W. Bush presidential china I had selected to go with my décor scheme. The Bush china is one of the most versatile services in the White House collection, featuring a beautiful green trellis-patterned border that is based on the historic Madison china. I felt that it was the perfect choice for my proposed plan for the India state dinner table décor. The butler then led me down to the vault that stored the priceless collection of 1,575 gilded 18th and 19th century French and English vermeil urns, bowls, candlesticks and vases that a collector named Margaret Thompson Biddle bequeathed to the White House in 1956. Here, I chose a footed pedestal vase for my state dinner centerpiece as well as four vermeil candlesticks. I felt giddy with excitement at the opportunity to incorporate such incredible pieces into my décor scheme. With my game plan, flower orders, container designs, and collateral material in place, I felt ready to compete.

The competition.

The following morning, competition day, I arrived at the White House entrance at 6:40 a.m. It was still pitch black outside and the temperature was cool with a hint of fall in the air. The guard checked my credentials and waved me on to the next checkpoint. Since we were allowed to bring our own containers and tools, the ushers had arranged for us to park close to the entrance on Upper East Executive Drive. After maneuvering through the multiple checkpoints, a flower shop staff member was standing there ready to meet me at the entrance.

White House staff delivered all of my supplies, containers and flowers to the Map Room, my appointed space. The other two finalists were working in the China Room and Vermeil Room on the other side of the Diplomatic Reception Room, all located on the ground floor of the White House adjacent to the Lower Cross Hall. We remained sequestered in these rooms throughout the competition. We did not interact at all and were not able to see each other's designs.

By the time my flowers and supplies were in place, it was already 7:30 a.m. We had about 3 ½ hours to complete everything. The mood felt very intense and the pressure was immense. I remember going in with a game plan and a sense of how I would pace myself but quickly lost track of time as the surreal scene unfolded around me. Initially, there was a flurry of activity with staff members scurrying in an out of the room, much like a scene from Downton Abbey. A butler set out coffee on the side table. Other butlers brought in the George W. Bush presidential china for my state dinner tableau and set the table with silver flatware. The curator delivered the special vermeil footed bowl that I had requested to use for the centerpiece design. I was instructed on how to handle it using white cotton gloves. Operations and paint shop staff put tarps on the floor and moved furniture out of the way. The carpenters adjusted the work tables to the perfect height. As everyone gradually left the room, I was able to concentrate and focus on the work in front of me.

My proposed tableau for the India state dinner was the most complicated project of the competition. This was my starting point. I soaked the floral foam for the vermeil centerpiece, placed the apple green silk cushion covers that matched the table linen on the chairs, and positioned the four vermeil candlesticks from the White House collection on the round table with eight place settings. I cut the flowers for the centerpiece design, which featured purple and fuchsia roses, purple orchids, sweet peas and hydrangea, and arranged them in a layered and textured garden style design. The finishing touch was purple clematis and pink jasmine vines that added movement and dimension in the bouquet. I also wrapped the candlesticks with vines and attached fuchsia orchids to resemble butterflies.

With this project complete, I moved on to the largest bouquet of the day – the Blue Room arrangement of blue and purple flowers. My technique for creating this large garden style design involved first establishing the structure and framework of the bouquet with branches and greenery. The next step was to add the focal point flower – hydrangea – as well as the main flower – the purple and lavender roses. After blocking in the basic shape with these elements, I layered in textures and accent blooms while rotating the design, alternating flowers and foliage to create the most natural effect and crossing stems to build depth and convey a sense of liveliness. The final step was to add movement to the piece by wrapping vines – in this case, passion flower vine – in and around the bouquet.

The final competition piece was the Oval Office arrangement. Using a contemporary distressed silver cube vase as the foundation of the design, I gathered an array of fall flowers and foliage for this bouquet: burgundy and green hydrangea, maple leaves, "liquid amber" foliage, rusty brown roses, rosehips and other berries. My color scheme was a rich, deep orange that I chose to complement the warm wood tones of the furnishings in the Oval Office. I checked the time and saw that I had a little under an hour to complete all of my displays. Looking around the Map Room, I couldn't believe how surreal it was to be part of this floral competition that seemed more suited for reality television than the White House.

Suddenly the door burst open, jolting me back to the reality of the moment. The housekeepers and operations crews had arrived to begin the clean-up process that signaled the end of the competition. Although I was basically done with my designs, I wanted to take one last look before the buckets of flowers were removed. I placed my brochures detailing my design philosophy on the table with the Blue Room display. The clean-up process was so efficient that within minutes the work room was dismantled and the historic furnishings were back in place.

After the crews left, I had a brief moment to gather my thoughts. It was very quiet and I could hear my heart pounding in my chest. Then the door knob turned again and an entourage of people entered the room, including the First Lady. It was so surprising to see her in person. I remember thinking how beautiful and lovely she looked. And she was very tall, towering over almost everyone else in the room. I appreciated how she immediately put me at ease with her warm and gracious welcome. 'Tell me what you've created here today,' she said smiling. I gave her one of my presentation brochures and started talking about the Blue Room arrangement, a large-scale bouquet created in the garden style. I explained that the garden style bouquet is the foundation of the new look for floral décor that I was proposing for the White House. It emphasizes the use of seasonal flowers, a broad and unusual combination of materials, and incorporates a modern design and color sense. It's a natural style that is both classic and elegant; an approach that is particularly appropriate for the White House where there is an intrinsic expectation of a refined style that complements the classical design and architecture. She was very attentive, asking me specific questions about the organic container and flowers that were used in this arrangement. She carried a small note pad on which she occasionally took notes. We spoke about the opportunity to introduce a new design aesthetic that could amplify her inspiring messages and policy agenda given the high profile and visibility of White House décor and flowers. I made the case that White House flowers could be deployed as an effective strategic communications tool – a new and exciting concept.

We moved on to the state dinner table display. I described the inspiration for the table and floral décor and how the choice of colors was designed to honor the special guests. I explained my technique of crossing stems and layering that created a lively and energetic feeling. The colors and shapes were modern; the use of the presidential china and vermeil incorporated and celebrated White House traditions. After all, this is what guests appreciate about experiencing a White House event, I noted, the opportunity to be at a table with these iconic symbols of American history and tradition. She commented on the flowers and vines that were wrapped around the candles, noting that she had never seen this technique before.

Next, we walked over to the Oval Office arrangement. I described the inspiration for the color scheme – the use of orange flowers and foliage to create a rich, autumn-themed bouquet. 'If I added blue flowers to this orange arrangement, it would be a Chicago Bears-themed bouquet,' I said, acknowledging the President's well-known affinity for his hometown sports team. She smiled and laughed, saying 'he would like that.'

The interview ended when an aide told the First Lady she needed to leave for her next meeting. Mrs. Obama thanked me for all of my hard work and said that she appreciated my participation in the contest. 'You're the local one, right?' she asked. 'Yes, I live here in the D.C. area, but I'm originally from Washington State.' She smiled, pointing to the sandwiches that the butlers had placed on the side table, urging me to eat some White House food before I left. 'You've worked hard, take a break,' she said.

After the group exited the room, I sat down for the first time all morning and nibbled on one of the sandwiches. It wasn't clear what would happen next. After what seemed like a long time, the Social Secretary and her assistant came back into the room. They were both smiling and beaming, offering congratulations on my presentation. They said that they loved the flowers. I thanked them for the opportunity to present my ideas, noting that the whole process had been an incredible experience and an honor. They said that they would be back in touch with me soon. I sat back down on the red silk Chippendale sofa and waited for what again seemed like another long period of time. Finally, the Chief Usher (the Admiral) came into the room. 'Well, you just blew the competition out of the water,' he said, congratulating me on my efforts. He told me that he had just finished meeting with the First Lady and her team. He hemmed and hawed for a moment as if unsure about what to say next. 'I'm pleased to tell you that you won the competition,' he finally blurted, 'but you can't tell anyone (except your husband).' Then he asked, 'when can you start?' He said the first official state dinner was a mere few weeks away and everyone was anxious for me to start as soon as possible.

I was so exhausted from the intensity of the competition (and early morning wake-up call) that it took a moment for reality to sink in. I had just won the competition to be the new Chief Floral Designer at the White House(!) I was shocked and stunned, but also felt extremely humbled and overcome with joy. This was the culmination of a seven or eight month-long interview process and years of study and hard work in floristry while simultaneously pursuing another career. He said that the Ushers' Office would be in touch with me about next steps for my security clearance and press announcement. The Admiral escorted me back to the flower shop area where I gathered up all of my things and loaded them into my car. As I drove away, I reflected on how lucky I was to live in such a great country that would allow my improbable ascent from my basement kitchen to the White House and the nation's top floral position. A land where if you work hard, dream big, and follow your passion, anything is possible.

AT THE WHITE HOUSE

FLORAL INSPIRATION

"YES WE CAN."

As everyone knows, President Obama's campaign slogan was "yes we can" and his inspirational message of "hope and change" emphasized bringing efficiency and best practices to every aspect of government. The Obamas made clear they wanted all Americans to experience the magical ambiance and historical significance of the White House as part of their strategy to strengthen the idea of the U.S. as a place of promise and possibility. They offered a transformational message of collaboration and cooperation, innovation and hope – the idea of harnessing American creativity and ingenuity to solve problems together, allowing everyone to reach higher towards the American dream. I saw how beautiful flowers could help convey that positive tone. During my interview, Mrs. Obama said she considered the flowers to be a very important part of White House life and wanted to continue the long-standing tradition of presenting beautiful displays in the White House state rooms as a way to honor visitors and special guests and add natural beauty to the historic rooms. The First Lady recognized the important symbolism of flowers as a way to communicate warmth, hospitality and a spirit of generosity. In this way, the flowers would create a strong and uplifting feeling, as well as set forth a spirit of classic and timeless American style.

At the White House, every aspect of style and décor is subject to intense scrutiny and debate, including the flowers. My goal was to elevate the discussion of flowers as simple decoration to the idea that they are actually a formidable policy tool. In the White House setting, I saw that the flowers could encompass more than just an aesthetic role. They can represent special themes, such as environmental, featuring natural containers and organic elements from the garden, highlighting conservation and sustainability. To emphasize culture, particular blooms and colors may be chosen to underscore traditions of visiting dignitaries, ensuring that flowers carry out a diplomatic role. Flowers also convey a symbolic message, exemplifying the essence of American style – friendly, accessible, warm, unexpected and fresh. My goal was to carry out the First Lady's vision of creating an inviting and welcoming ambiance for all guests and visitors, whether they were presidents of foreign countries or American families visiting the White House from across the country. At the nation's most visible and important address, I envisioned incorporating new trends in floral artistry in White House designs with the goal of showcasing a distinctly American vision of contemporary floral style.

Mrs. Obama clearly wanted the flowers to reflect her personal style and priorities. By then, the First Lady had captured the world's imagination with the planting of the White House kitchen garden and its public policy connection to a healthy lifestyle and diet, single-handedly launching a surge in the popularity of gardening. In our meeting, we discussed how the garden-style of flower arranging -- involving flowers loosely arranged in overlapping layers and placed in natural, organic containers -- would help carry out her message – and bring the garden inside. In addition to flowers, the garden style also features elements such as fruits and vegetables that are incorporated into arrangements, which would be another way to link a new design aesthetic with her signature "Let's Move" program. It struck me that her vision was similar to former First Lady Jackie Kennedy's view that the White House should be decorated with fresh flowers that appear as if they had been cut from the garden, arranged casually in an English country house style, based on Dutch and Flemish paintings, radiating a casual, yet elegant flair.

The First Lady had also become a trend-setting fashion icon, introducing a new and modern style of dressing that centered around mixing high end designer clothes with well-known retail brands such as J.Crew and The Gap. During my interview, we spoke about how this concept could apply to White House floral design as well. By using a combination of humble garden flowers with special accents such as cattelaya orchids or gloriosa lilies, it would be possible to create elegant yet accessible (and budget-conscious) designs. A fresh approach of combining flowers and colors would create a subtle, yet modern take on traditional White House floral designs, and result in a new and very personal signature style.

Building on this theme, we discussed how a new style and fresh approach to the flower program would support her vision and be reflective of her overall sense of style – one that is modern, thoughtful, vibrant, and quintessentially American. It was exciting to contemplate a fresh, innovative floral outlook to what promised to be a fresh, innovative presidential administration. The concept involved introducing several new elements: a new aesthetic style, a new way of working (with expanded hours and more volunteers), a new approach for sourcing materials (emphasizing local farms and American-grown flowers), and innovative ways of using flowers as a communications tool that were in sync with the administration's priorities. The goal was to introduce a timeless, natural floral aesthetic that embraced new techniques and created a look of casual elegance using flowers from American landscapes: woodlands, meadows, fields, vineyards and gardens.

THE GARDEN STYLE

The garden style bouquet, as Jackie Kennedy originally envisioned, is the foundation of the new look for floral décor that I brought to the White House in 2009. It emphasizes the use of seasonal flowers, a broad and unusual combination of materials, and incorporates a modern design and color sense. It is a natural style that is particularly appropriate for the White House where there is an intrinsic expectation of a refined and elegant approach befitting the classical design and architecture. Here are the basic elements of the garden style approach.

A solid theme. A beautiful bouquet starts with a strong artistic vision. The concept defines every element of the bouquet from container to flowers to the finishing touches to ensure a cohesive presentation and overall look. For example, a starting point of inspiration could be a "secret garden" bouquet of romantic garden roses, trailing vines and ferns gathered in an organic leaf-covered container. The romantic theme is translated through choice of elements and the mood it creates. Or, an arrangement could re-present a particular season – an early spring bouquet of jonquils with pussy willow branches or an autumn-themed bouquet of mums and rosehips. The essential characteristics of each season are distilled in the floral choices and design techniques. Another approach is to evoke a special landscape, such as a Provencal bouquet of sunflowers, wheat and lavender or a Pacific Northwest bouquet of rhododendron, moss and ferns. The completed bouquet should transport the viewer to that special place. By envisioning an inspiring theme and mapping out the details, it's possible to create a design with emotional impact that resonates.

A structured shape. The second element of the garden style approach is to create a structured round shape that is the foundation of the design. The addition of escaping elements, including flowers and vines, is important for adding movement and dimension as well as a sense of whimsy. The first step is to create a base for the flowers, using a fairly dense structure of greens. One technique I use is to arrange base greenery in concentric circles with crossed stems to create underlying movement. This automatically creates a dynamic garden-style look and ensures that the bouquet will retain its shape and last longer. The next step is to add flowers to develop the structured round shape – the classic *bouquet rond* – a classical French form that is contemporary and chic, working in planes, creating depth and movement in the design.

An integrated container. A third special attribute of the garden style bouquet is an organic container that integrates the overall design concept, linking the base with the flowers to create an entire artistic presentation and a cohesive design concept. The container becomes its own artistic element that can be made from folded leaves, dried fruits, woven grasses, etc. to create an endless variety of patterns and motifs that coordinate with the bouquet. These containers give a very natural feel to the design, as if the flowers are growing out of the base.

A strong sense of color. Color is the next essential consideration in the garden style. My general rule of thumb is to follow the colors that grow together in the garden for each season. Monochromatic color schemes are a good starting point for design – the idea of using varying shades of the same hue to create visual impact and drama. Another approach is to blend two complementary colors – purple and green, orange and blue, red and green, but in doses that are not half and half. It's better to create a purple bouquet with a few green accents (or vice versa) than to divide the colors in a half and half display. White flowers (offset with foliage in every shade of green) are always an elegant choice. One interesting technique is to use the flowers themselves as the inspiration point for color combinations. By taking a petal and studying its many variations in colors and hues, and then choosing flowers in that color palette, it's possible to develop sophisticated and complex color schemes that go beyond predictable combinations to create surprising results: coral with lavender and burgundy, gold with bronze and plum, pink with peach and coral. Using a technique of flower petals as clues, interesting and inspiring colors can help achieve evocative results.

A mixed composition. The fifth essential element of the garden style is the mixing of unusual components, colors and textures, including fruits, flowers, vegetables and foliage. The contemporary garden style is based on the assumption that all elements of nature are equal – from the humble grasses and woodland pods, to the garden roses and vine tomatoes, to exotic orchids and rare fruits – and that a bouquet should represent a full landscape of these ephemeral elements to add poetry and emotional impact to designs. Ideally, a composition should have a mix of shapes such as round roses, textured hydrangea, a star-shaped gloriosa lily, and a spray of berries. A recipe I use when creating a bouquet involves five key elements: a large focal point flower, main flower, accent flower, texture, and finishing touches.

A refined technique. A few techniques are key for achieving the garden style aesthetic. These techniques, including swirling greenery, crossing stems, and layering of materials to help achieve a look that is at once both natural and sophisticated. The layers of depth and complexity of design create a liveliness in the bouquet that is interesting and exciting. The goal is to visualize a sense of lightness from within – as if the bouquet is springing out of the container. All of these techniques are designed to create a feeling of being in the garden – the windswept vines, shaggy ferns, and different heights and depths of flowers. It is this feeling of energy and lightness that defines the garden style.

Finishing touches. The final distinguishing element of the garden style is the finishing touch – the intricate and couture style techniques that focus on creativity and innovation as well as on creating movement and a sense of liveliness with dancing branches, floating butterfly orchids, wrapping vines and ferns, ribbons, grasses, etc. – that add finesse and elegance to the overall arrangements. Finishing touches also add dimension and depth to the designs. I always try to avoid stiff or formulaic approaches in the garden style since the primary emphasis should be on creativity and originality in every piece.

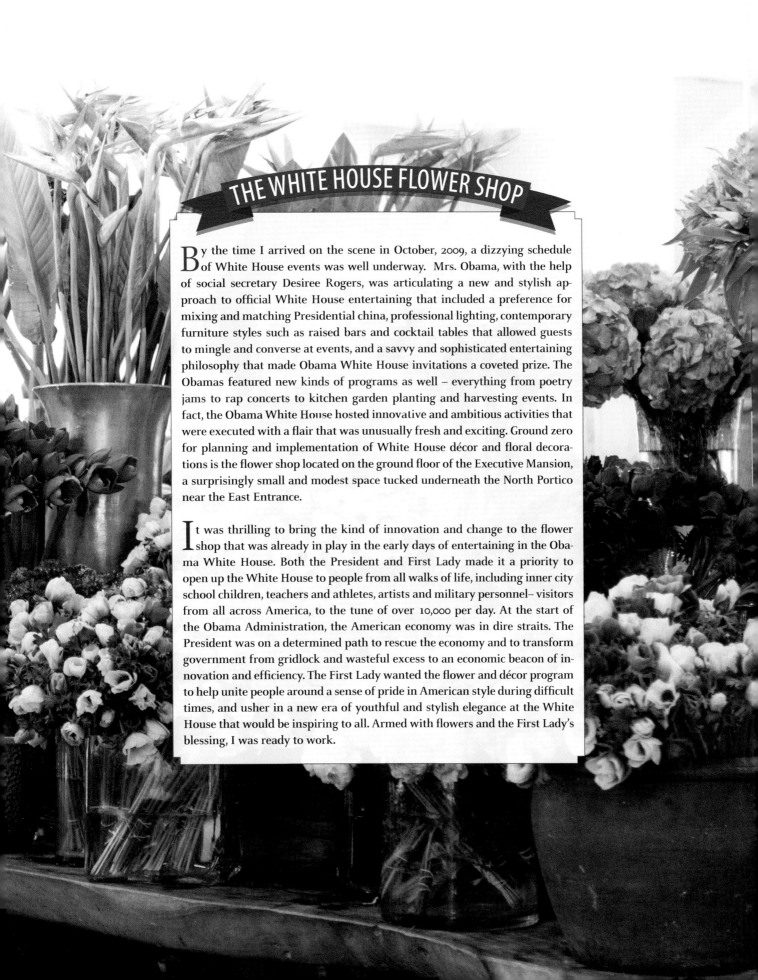

THE WHITE HOUSE FLOWER SHOP

By the time I arrived on the scene in October, 2009, a dizzying schedule of White House events was well underway. Mrs. Obama, with the help of social secretary Desiree Rogers, was articulating a new and stylish approach to official White House entertaining that included a preference for mixing and matching Presidential china, professional lighting, contemporary furniture styles such as raised bars and cocktail tables that allowed guests to mingle and converse at events, and a savvy and sophisticated entertaining philosophy that made Obama White House invitations a coveted prize. The Obamas featured new kinds of programs as well – everything from poetry jams to rap concerts to kitchen garden planting and harvesting events. In fact, the Obama White House hosted innovative and ambitious activities that were executed with a flair that was unusually fresh and exciting. Ground zero for planning and implementation of White House décor and floral decorations is the flower shop located on the ground floor of the Executive Mansion, a surprisingly small and modest space tucked underneath the North Portico near the East Entrance.

It was thrilling to bring the kind of innovation and change to the flower shop that was already in play in the early days of entertaining in the Obama White House. Both the President and First Lady made it a priority to open up the White House to people from all walks of life, including inner city school children, teachers and athletes, artists and military personnel– visitors from all across America, to the tune of over 10,000 per day. At the start of the Obama Administration, the American economy was in dire straits. The President was on a determined path to rescue the economy and to transform government from gridlock and wasteful excess to an economic beacon of innovation and efficiency. The First Lady wanted the flower and décor program to help unite people around a sense of pride in American style during difficult times, and usher in a new era of youthful and stylish elegance at the White House that would be inspiring to all. Armed with flowers and the First Lady's blessing, I was ready to work.

In order to make the requested stylistic adjustments in flowers and decor, it was obvious we couldn't go about business as usual. The First Lady's vision required a change in style, business practices and work philosophy. It meant transforming the flower shop from an outdated government operation to an innovative environment with a business start-up mentality and entrepreneurial approach. In early 2010, I launched a flower shop planning process designed to articulate a fresh strategic direction. Inspired by the Obama Administration's focus on transforming government, I followed suit, making several operational changes designed to increase quality, efficiency and effectiveness. We extended flower shop hours, re-aligned staffing schedules, redefined roles and responsibilities, brought in expertise from other areas, expanded the volunteer program and created a professional, project-based work model that eliminated excessive overtime costs. We started by crafting ambitious vision and mission statements, followed by a specific set of goals and objectives that supported them:

Vision statement. To create an innovative, professional, world class operation focusing on leading-edge floral artistry that carries out the First Lady's vision of implementing a new signature White House garden style.

Mission statement. To provide high quality floral design and décor for the entire White House portfolio: 1) state and ground floors for public tours, 2) private residence, 3) east and west wing offices, and 4) White House events including dinners, receptions, state dinners, etc. To plan, coordinate, and execute major design projects, including the White House Christmas, working collaboratively with internal and external partners, fully integrating current resources with expanded volunteer networks.

A key part of the plan involved expanding the number of strategic partnerships to increase our capacity to produce high-quality designs. There was already a long-standing tradition of bringing volunteers to the White House to assist with holiday decorating and major events such as the 4th of July. But I saw an immediate opportunity to use volunteers on an everyday basis. With volunteer support, we dramatically increased the number of hours devoted to floral art and White House design – at zero additional cost. We also increased the level of

specialized expertise through the volunteer program, inviting talented artists to contribute to a wide variety of projects. Sometimes, it went well beyond floral design to encompass broader needs: graphic design, event planning and design, architectural rendering, and even robotics. Through the volunteer program, we created a depth of talent that was truly inspirational. All of these talented artists were extremely proud to share their creative achievements on the prestigious White House stage.

One of my all-time favorite volunteer collaborations was with a local sugar artist and cake baker who hand-crafted iconic sugar flower vases for my holiday floral displays. These beautiful vases, involving countless hours of painstakingly detailed work, each took her over six months to complete. They were a highlight of White House holiday décor and left an indelible impression on everyone who saw them. They are exquisite proof of the importance and value of volunteers at the White House.

In addition to these specialized contributions, there were florists who worked with me in the trenches and behind the scenes who contributed to White House floral diplomacy. Early on in my tenure, we brought in networks of florists and designers from across the country to assist with the full range of flower shop duties – from processing flowers and sweeping floors to designing bouquets and creating intricately patterned organic vases. Over the years, the program expanded to include garden clubs, free-lance floral designer networks, and representatives from the American Institute of Floral Designers (AIFD), the professional group of highly trained florists – the floral equivalency of a special operations unit heading into an important mission.

Without exception, all of these volunteers brought an incredible spirit of positive energy every time they visited me at the White House, a can-do spirit of excellence, achievement and patriotism that was delightful and contagious. To this day, I am grateful for their many contributions to the White House flower program. I credit them for expanding the boundaries beyond anything we could have otherwise achieved given budget and staffing constraints. They helped us realize some of our most ambitious and memorable design projects – and created some of our most beautiful work.

A TYPICAL DAY

My work schedule can best be described as intense and grueling – 16 hour days, 100 hour work weeks, 7 days a week for 6 years. Early on, I understood that to make a real difference and to carry out the First Lady's vision, I would need to put in extraordinary hours – and bring others in to work alongside me. Luckily, I had the stamina and motivation (as well as knowledge from my marathon days on how to pace myself) to work this schedule. My typical work day started at home around 6 a.m. with a check of my Blackberry to see what had transpired overnight or was already on the day's agenda. After a morning run (time to clear my head and come up with new ideas), I stopped by my favorite coffee shop to grab two large cups of coffee on my way in to the White House. I usually arrived at my desk between 8:30 a.m. and 9 a.m. By then, the flower shop routines were in full swing – the daily maintenance routines and flower deliveries throughout the White House complex –and I could check in with my team on any updates or issues that required my attention. This was a busy time of day, with meetings and new project assignments, impromptu visits and requests from West Wing and East Wing staffers, staff briefings and guidance for volunteers . . . with the phone always ringing in the background.

There were always at least 10 different activities occurring at once, from administrative and management tasks (ordering flowers, managing routines, developing budgets and cost projections, creating work plans and staffing schedules) to creative jobs (designing bouquets, creating event inspiration boards, crafting design prototypes and organic containers, etc.), involving a variety of different timelines and deadlines. For example, the planning for the White House Christmas was a year-round project that was an ongoing part of my daily schedule – whether it was initial note-taking and concept development in January and February, organizing the warehouse in March, writing proposals in April and May, creating prototypes and room by room plans in the summer to intense project management in the fall as we inched closer to the installation date. Other projects, including state dinners, Governors' Dinners and major events like 4th of July or Halloween, usually had a 3 or 4 month lead time to plan and implement. In addition to décor plans, these complex events involved meetings about logistics, security and protocol requirements. Some events would be added to the calendar without much notice or lead time; we built these into our timelines and plans. In addition to the non-stop event portfolio, I managed the daily and weekly flower installations for the East and West Wing offices, State Floors, and private residence – and even Camp David when the First Family decamped there for periodic escapes.

By midday, after the morning routines were completed, we turned our focus to that day's events – setting up flowers and décor for luncheons, receptions, meetings or dinners that were taking place within the White House complex. Later in the afternoon, volunteers joined me to work on special projects – creating organic containers, intricate holiday designs and helping with general flower shop tasks. It was also a time to catch up on e-mails and other administrative work as well as to complete the constant flow of bouquets that were part of my daily responsibility. At the conclusion of White House events, we would break down the event, removing flowers from the state floor (or south lawn, West Wing, or wherever the event was held) and return them to the cooler. The "night shift" continued until 8 or 9 p.m., concluding with a clean-up and sweep of the flower shop to get everything ready for the next day.

My White House work continued at home into the evening. After a quick dinner with my husband, I worked on flower orders, proposals and creative research until about midnight when I called it a day, my mind still buzzing with the check lists, deadlines and details of my White House job. It was both an incredibly demanding and immensely rewarding position – and I enjoyed every minute of it!.

THE WHITE HOUSE OFFICIAL EVENTS

DIPLOMATIC & POLITICAL

THE FIRST STATE DINNER

When I first arrived at the White House in October 2009, the India state dinner, the first of the Obama Administration, was less than a month away. Although some planning was already underway, including plans to erect a large tent on the South Lawn to accommodate over 400 people, the actual décor for the event and the tables had yet to be finalized. The Social Secretary, Desiree Rogers, arranged for a special décor viewing with the First Lady in the private residence in early November. The objective was to present options for linens, china and flowers – including the winning design I created for my competition. With assistance from the butlers, two distinct tables were set with linens, china, chairs, flowers and candles in the Yellow Oval Room. One concept was beautiful and understated: a white linen table cloth topped with cream gold-rimmed (rental) china and accented with a bouquet of amber-colored orchids and roses. I also recreated my competition look inspired by the colors of the Indian peacock: apple green silk linen, the George W. Bush china, and a centerpiece made of purple and fuchsia flowers – hydrangea, sweet peas, roses and orchids – displayed in the Tiffany bamboo gold centerpieces first selected by former First Lady Jacqueline Kennedy. The First Lady was drawn to the more colorful display and once again selected my "Indian peacock" theme for the dinner.

With less than a few weeks to carry out this much-antici-pated event, we swung into an intense period of planning. Details like the matching green silk cushion covers for the chairs had to be ordered, along with the amethyst-colored water glasses that would coordinate with the fuchsia and purple centerpiece designs. Since the event was so large and taking place outside of the White House, we needed to augment the Vermeil bamboo floral containers and candlesticks that were already on hand (part of the historic White House collection) with additional pieces. I researched options for the table settings along with identify-ing the large urns from the White House collection that would hold massive displays of cut magnolia branches. To elevate these arran-gements in the gigantic tent, the in-house carpenters built 14 wood pedestal bases which were painted a soft shade of dove gray. Additional planning requirements included ordering all of the flowers, developing the staffing and work plans for the days leading up to the event and finalizing the supplies and materials. To create the feeling of a secret garden, we embellished huge vintage chandeliers from the Nixon era (discovered in the off-site storage facility) by wrapping them with long strands of ivy. These were hung from the top of the tent. The tent floors were covered in a wheat-colored carpet; the tent walls were lined with a deep, emerald green velvet. A lighting designer provided professional lighting for the tent décor, which created a beautiful ambiance, illuminating the centerpieces and the mag-nolia branch displays. In addition to the flowers for the state dinner itself, I was responsible for creating arrangements for all of the White House state rooms as well as the floral décor for the private reception the President and First Lady hosted in the Yel-low Oval Room before the event.

The social office organized a press preview the day before the actual event, hosted by the First Lady. This is a longstanding White House tradition that involves inviting members of the national and international press to the White House to see the table settings, hear about the menu selection, and receive a briefing from the West Wing team on highlights of the bi-lateral relationship. I remember peeking through a crack in the Old Family Dining room door as the press scrum rushed into the State Dining Room. They literally raced to the tables that were completely set with flowers, linens, china and silverware, cameras and equipment in tow, jostling and elbowing their way to be the first ones to capture the first image of the Obamas' first state dinner.

For the press packet, I provided notes on the décor to the First Lady's communications team that described the inspiration for the color scheme and choice of flowers as well as details about the flowers we used. The flowers (roses, hydrangea and sweet peas) in shades of deep plum, purple and fuchsia were designed to evoke the classic American garden. The magnolia branches, native to both the U.S. and India, were locally grown and sustainably harvested. Thus, through the choice of colors, types of flowers and source of materials, we were able to convey both national symbolism as well as environmental themes. The approach seemed to capture the imagination of the press who reported extensively on these "modern" choices.

The night of the dinner was pure magic. As the State Dinner guests arrived, they entered via the East Wing entrance, walking along the East Colonnade up the stairs to the receiving line with the President and First Lady in the Blue Room. From there, they descended the Blue Room balcony stairs to a covered walkway that was lit with candles and flowers floating in tall cylinder vases before entering the main tent that glowed in vivid shades of apple green, fuchsia and purple. Later that night, Desiree told me that the guests were spell-bound by the décor and ambiance that we had created. She said that many guests regularly attend glittery black tie events on both coasts but found this state dinner experience to be especially beautiful, as if they had entered a secret, magical garden that was transformed with twinkling candlelight and inspirational colors and flowers. Of course, the evening's entertainment – featuring Indian Bollywood dancers wearing colorful costumes and Academy Award-winning singer Jennifer Hudson – not to mention the incredible meal created by celebrity guest chef Marcus Samuelson – contributed to the evening's spectacular success.

For one day, we basked in the feeling of accomplishment of our collective efforts and celebrated the results of our work. And then the bizarre tale of two reality television stars who brazenly made their way inside the White House and all of the way down to the tent in a shocking security breach began to unfold – forever changing the narrative about that first state dinner. Nevertheless, the India State Dinner was by far my favorite of all of the Obama state dinners I worked on, combining modern décor elements with cherished White House traditions, bold colors and clear symbolism that honored both the visiting guests and our American heritage. It was a wonderful evening of floral diplomacy.

MEXICO STATE DINNER

The Obama Administration's second state dinner with Mexico in May, 2010, presented another great opportunity for floral diplomacy. With so much rich history, culture and tradition to draw upon to highlight the connections between our two countries, we set out to weave an enchanting tale of beauty and inspiration in all of the floral details. The dinner in honor of Mexican President Calderon and First Lady Margarita Zavala was held in the East Room for 220 guests, followed by dessert and a reception in a tent for 400 people on the South Lawn, and capped off with a special performance by international superstar Beyonce. The color scheme for the dinner – fuchsia and turquoise – was inspired by nature and Mexican cultural tradition, the colors of the Mayan sun and sea gods, and carried out in the table settings and floral décor. The boldly striped table linens were made in three hues of turquoise blue, resembling rippling ocean waves, an elegant backdrop for the gold-rimmed Clinton and Eisenhower service plates at each table setting. The floral designs for the dinner included many individual layers of symbolism starting with the hand-made gilded baskets that were woven in Mexico, a nod to their tradition of artistry and craftsmanship. We filled the baskets with fuchsia, plum and pale lilac flowers, including fragrant Yves Piaget garden roses, cattelaya orchids and passionflower vines.

A special element in each bouquet was the prickly pear cactus – a beautiful lavender-toned cactus plant indigenous to Mexico that we sourced from a supplier in Las Vegas, Nevada, appropriately named "Cactus Joe." I still remember the hilarious scene that unfolded when the boxes of prickly pear cactus arrived in the flower shop. Eager staff and volunteers tore open the boxes, reaching in to grab the cactus – and then immediately regretted the decision since their hands were now covered in thousands of prickly pear spines that stung and burned beyond belief. "Quick, quick," someone shouted, "let's get Cactus Joe on the line and get an antidote!" I don't remember Cactus Joe's exact advice, but I think it had something to do with soaking hands in a mix of milk and Miracle Whip until the burning sensation subsided. In retrospect, it occurs to me that the prickly pear cactus – albeit a perfect symbolic choice of floral material – was also quite risky. What if an unsuspecting guest inadvertently reached across the table to admire the flowers only to be blindsided by a handful of prickly and painful cactus spines?

The vision of a near-miss international incident at a previous state dinner with Mexico crossed my mind. For that event during the George W. Bush Administration, the White House pastry chef concocted an elaborate dessert featuring a traditional hacienda and a Mexican man lounging under a large sombrero. As the chefs prepared to serve the dessert, the political staff became alarmed at what could be construed as an unflattering cultural stereotype. At the last minute, they plucked the little sombrero-wearing figurine from each plate before the waiters entered the room, averting a crisis (but perhaps compromising the dessert's aesthetic presentation).

Luckily for me, there were no mishaps that night, and when it came time to dismantle the cactus arrangements, we imported a special team of tough guys from Brooklyn who wore layers of protective leather gloves to handle them. Suffice it to say that the prickly pear cactus motif was a one-time White House design! In the private residence, the preparations for the Mexico state visit were equally elaborate. On the morning of the State Dinner, while the state arrival ceremony was underway on the White House South Lawn, featuring Presidential speeches, a review of troops, and traditional American fife and drum music, we delivered the flowers for the private reception that would be held that evening to the second floor private residence. Here, the President and First Lady would receive President Calderon and Mrs. Zavala, as well as other notables, including the Secretary of State and Vice President and Dr. Jill Biden. Our floral task involved covering almost every surface with a floral arrangement. Once again, I looked to nature and Mexican culture and tradition for inspiration. My starting point was the containers. I used a mix of hand-crafted organic vessels made of woven leaves and grasses in the Mexican tradition of textile weaving and basketry, incorporating Mexican-inspired patterns and motifs, along with Vermeil urns and porcelain bowls from the White House collection. We also used a mix of fruit and flowers to honor the agricultural traditions and natural beauty of Mexico. One arrangement featured a vase made of fresh limes, one of the biggest export items of Mexico. Additional pieces included topiary designs crafted out of Mexican heather – the feathery purple flower native from Mexico to Honduras that is attractive to hummingbirds and butterflies – as well as brightly colored pots of early summer blooms that were inspired by renowned Mexican folk artist Frida Kahlo. Each bouquet was an opportunity to honor and engage the Mexican President and First Lady with designs referencing familiar examples of Mexican art, landscapes and culture. The flowers served as mini floral ambassadors that as a collection created a welcoming environment and beautiful ambiance for the visiting Mexican delegation.

In the Center Hall, I created a large display inspired by Mayan art, architecture and cultural achievements. The large center-piece bouquet in shades of Mayan blue and purple was designed to resemble the structure and symmetry of Mayan ruins. The Center Hall bouquets are always displayed on a 19th century octagonal partners' desk that sits in the center point of the long hall, directly above the main Cross Hall below. For the Mexico state dinner, we surrounded the main bouquet with earthy pots of baby tears and maidenhair ferns.

The reception tent on the South Lawn contained some of the most elaborate and beautiful décor of all. The tent walls were lined with black velvet fabric to create a romantic jewel box interior. Thousands of paper monarch butterflies and crystal garlands were hung from the ceiling on a gossamer thread to appear as if they were floating in the space. The monarch butterfly décor was designed to honor President Calderon and his birthplace of Michoacan, Mexico, the origin of the butterfly's annual migration to Canada each year, a perfect symbol of international dialogue and cooperation. We created table decorations of dried apricot vases that were filled with herbs, a natural and organic touch that complemented the butterfly theme.

That night I was invited to come down to the South Lawn tent to see the post-State Dinner program unfold. I put on a long black gown and heels and headed to the reception from the Executive Mansion. When I walked down the White House drive, which was lit by lanterns and decorated with flowers, I found the effect to be breathtakingly magical. The majestic trees on the grounds were illuminated by spotlights, their silhouettes casting dancing shadows across the grounds. As I entered the tent, I saw how the orange butterflies floated and sparkled against the velvety black backdrop with the large hanging baskets of flowers and greenery adding a secret garden feeling to the space. Cocktail tables surrounded by banquette seating areas at different levels created an intimate, club-like ambiance. When Beyonce came on stage for an acoustic performance, the mood in the tent was electric. At one point during her set, I looked down at my watch – it was getting late and I still had flower arrangements to finish before the next day. In a move like Cinderella, I ran back to the flower shop, exchanging my gown for my work outfit, with visions of bouquets, butterflies – and Beyonce – inspiring my late night designs.

At the 2016 North American Leaders' summit, President Obama referenced the journey of the butterfly across North America, observing that it is a symbol of strength, perseverance and international cooperation – a perfect example of nature's diplomacy.

GERMANY STATE DINNER

In June, 2011, the President and First Lady hosted German Chancellor Angela Merkel and her husband for a lavish state dinner in the Rose Garden. As part of the planning process before the event, we set up a décor preview in the Rose Garden – three different table settings and floral designs from which the First Lady could choose. While we were debating the merits of various options and color schemes as the First Lady pondered the different choices, a surprise guest joined us in the Rose Garden. The President emerged from the Oval Office with a football under his arm that he playfully threw back and forth to social office staff. "You all look like you're having way too much fun out here," he said. By then, the First Family's dog Bo had also joined in on the impromptu football game. After a while, the First Lady turned to the President and jokingly said, "this is my territory, now get back to work." It was a fun, lighthearted moment – which was also somewhat surreal. Eventually, the First Lady selected a bright summery theme for this outdoor state dinner: shimmery white sequined table cloths topped by yellow and green floral arrangements and the Bush presidential china. Additional accents of floating candles, silver-rimmed votives and silver metal garden chairs completed the elegant décor.

In researching ways to make the flowers meaningful and tie them in to the Germany state visit, I was inspired by Angela Merkel's lofty academic achievements. She holds a doctorate in quantum chemi-cal physics, an amazing feat. This was my starting point for developing the décor in the private residence where the President and First Lady would host the couple for a small reception. Using science as inspiration, I created a focal point display for the Center Hall that incorporated the infinity motif and surrounded the main bouquet with topiaries that represented molecular structures. Here are the notes I provided for the First Lady's briefing book regarding that display:

The Quantum Chemistry Bouquets
Presented by Chief Floral Designer, Laura Dowling

"In honor of Chancellor Merkel's academic and professional achievements, we created a Center Hall floral presentation that celebrates principles of quantum chemistry, an area in which Dr. Merkel received her doctoral degree with a dissertation entitled "Theoretical Approach to Reactions of Polyatomic Molecules."

Quantum chemistry applies quantum mechanics to the explanation and prediction of chemical behavior. The first step in solving a quantum chemical problem is usually solving the Schrödinger equation and determining the electronic structure of the molecule. The four small topiary displays surrounding the main bouquet, made of moss, horsetail and lily grass depict stylized molecular structures, and are displayed in geometric cube vases

wrapped in green leaves. The lily grass inside the cube represents the symbol for infinity – the idea of an infinite amount of particles and molecules in the universe. Infinity means "always and forever" and is a powerful symbol of limitless, never-ending possibilities."

For additional design inspiration, I researched Dr. Merkel's favorite color – yellow – and explored her interest in cooking and baking. I learned that she is well-known for her potato soup and beef loaf recipes, and especially for making her famous plum cake. In the Yellow Oval Room arrangements, I tucked plum-colored flowers and fruit into the yellow bouquets, a reference to her signature confection, with the goal of creating another opportunity for conversation and floral diplomacy.

As I put the final finishing touches on the arrangements in the Rose Garden that afternoon, American singer James Taylor was practicing his classic hit "You've Got a Friend" which he would perform for the guests later that evening. Through color, composition, and background research, we created a richly textured, highly nuanced, and very personal collection of floral art displays in honor of Chancellor Merkel – a perfect setting for a state dinner with one of our closest European allies.

After the set-up for the state dinner was complete, I ironically raced to catch a flight to Germany where I was scheduled to take part in an annual international flower class with talented florists from throughout the world. It was truly a day of floral diplomacy on every level.

FLORAL DIPLOMACY
THE OFFICIAL FLORIST

Through my flower studies in Europe and speaking engage-ments across the country, I've had the opportunity to meet talented colleagues from around the world who hold "official" florist positions similar to my former White House job. It's always fascinating to compare notes about our positions – the scope of work in official settings, stylistic and cultural preferences, staffing, budgets and other details – and to discuss both the striking similarities and major differences in these jobs. We all operate under intense scrutiny and pressure, producing highly visible work in fast-paced and constantly evolving environments – in venerable venues where history was made and continues to un-fold. We create flowers that are accessories to diplomacy, visual symbols of national identity and culture. Although most offi-cial florists are subject to strict budgetary constraints, there are some exceptions. The royal florist of a Middle Eastern country, for example, manages a team of 150 florists who create lavish bouquets for the Sultan's palaces each day, including floating flowers for the pools. A few years ago, he and his colleagues were on a six week training trip with European master florists, a luxuri-ous investment in talent.

While official flower budgets may vary from country to country, all official florists understand the need for utmost discretion in these jobs, especially when it involves dealing with high profile events and heads of state. A talented British colleague designed the flowers for the royal fairytale wedding of Prince William and Kate Middleton, the ultimate celebrity event requiring the kind of tight-lipped silence surrounding flowers (and especially her bridal bouquet) that would have made James Bond proud. In some countries, flowers are an intrinsic part of national and cultural identity. A Belgian florist friend was recently honored to be among a handful of artists invited to have dinner with the Queen of Belgium, a major show of support and acknowledgement of the country's achievements in floristry and a testament to the Queen's personal interest in Belgian artists and their work.

As a French-trained florist and Francophile, I was thrilled by the opportunity to tour the Elysse Palace in Paris, the official residence of the President of the French Republic, twice in recent years. A friend and colleague organized private tours of the kitchen, flower shop, wine cellar, china room, and silver vault – incredible, behind-the-scenes glimpses into centuries of French official style and entertaining. The historic collections of hand-painted Sevres and Limoges porcelain are exceptionally beautiful and made a big impression on me. These *décorations de table*, featuring intricate patterns of birds and flowers, landscape scenes and geometric motifs are triumphs of artistic achievement as well as cherished symbols of French history and tradition. I was surprised to learn that although the porcelain pieces are priceless and irreplaceable, they are often used for official state events. The French official in charge of the collection graciously retrieved the pieces for us to see and described historic events where they were used. For one especially beautiful official visit that was held in the *Salle de Fêtes* (Hall of Festivities), bouquets of ombre-hued French garden roses spanned the table end to end, presented in hand-painted antique Sevres vases to create an undulating sea of color, ranging from blush pink to deep burgundy red, that perfectly complemented the rich tapestries, carpets and silk draperies in the room.

When I entered the flower shop at the Elysse Palace, there was a definite sense of *déjà vu*. The physical space was amazingly similar to the White House flower shop and even the staff set-up was exactly the same– one Chief Floral Designer and three full-time support staff. Because the Elysse Palace is not open to the public (except one day a year), the flowers are used only in the private spaces and for official events. During my tour, a designer was making small cubes of individual flowers that were lit up by LED lights. He said that then-President Sarkozy favored this type of simple, modern arrangement for his dinner table. There were also scores of elegant bouquets stored in the cooler ready for delivery and placement in the private apartments. At the time, the Sarkozys' flower budget was under scrutiny. Press reports said that First Lady Carla Bruni was racking up the equivalent of over a half million dollars in annual floral expenses, in what was criticized as a very Marie Antoinette-like level of extravagant taste and style. Although these reports were inaccurate according to my French floral colleagues, the Sarkozys clearly loved flowers and appreciated having them in their home.

FRANCE VISIT
PRESIDENT SARKOZY

A highlight of my tenure at the White House was the privilege of creating flowers and décor for two France state visits. In late March 2010, President and Mrs. (Carla Bruni) Sarkozy visited the White House for an (unofficial) private dinner with the Obamas. The French first couple had first hosted the newly elected President and First Lady in Paris early in 2009 and this was an opportunity to reciprocate. The guests enjoyed a dinner in the Yellow Oval Room in the private residence. Although the event was small and intimate, occurring outside of press coverage and the public eye – a great deal of thought went into the planning and orchestration of the evening. From the moment the first couple of France arrived at the North Portico, to the cocktail hour on the Truman Balcony, to the elegant dinner in the Yellow Oval Room, the evening was a perfect blend of floral, culinary and design diplomacy. In preparation for the evening, many of the special French décor elements – elaborate 18th century candelabra, gilded vases, ormolu lamps – and the piece de resistance – the exquisite Monroe Plateau – a *surtout de table* (a gold-gilt bronze mirrored centerpiece) were retrieved from White House storage and put on display. The plateau, which was acquired during President Monroe's 1817 renovation of the White House, is especially beautiful when it's filled with flowers and candles that are reflected in the 7 mirrored, footed platforms of the 14 ft. long piece. That night, it featured bouquets of pink parrot tulips and French garden roses arranged in the plateau's coordinating gilded vases and baskets, and was illuminated by candles that glittered on the mirrored display.

For the dinner in the private residence, I created flowers that were inspired by the *Jardin des Tuileries* in Paris. This iconic garden is only a short distance away from the Élysée Palace, the home of the French First Family, and I envisioned that they undoubtedly spent time there, strolling through the lovely gardens that extend from the base of the Champs-Élysées to the Palace of the Louvre. No matter what time of year, the gardens exude a timeless beauty with large topiary bay leaf trees, marble statuary, fountains and flowers – an idyllic and tranquil oasis in the middle of Paris. For the arrangements in the Center Hall, the first space that visitors see after they embark from the elevator on the second floor, I chose seasonal flowers that were inspired by these gardens: Yves Piaget garden roses (a fragrant deep fuchsia variety) with French lilacs and trailing jasmine vines crafted into classic topiary shapes – a hallmark of the French garden aesthetic.

Although it was still early in the spring season, the Obamas wanted to host their guests for a cocktail hour on the Truman Balcony with its unparalleled view of the South Lawn, the Washington monument and the Lincoln Memorial. It truly is a spectacular place for a cocktail reception. However, just that winter, Washington, D.C. had been inundated with an epic snowstorm, nicknamed "Snowmageddon," which dumped over 3 ft. of snow in the region and paralyzed the city for weeks. The early spring flowers were several weeks behind their typical bloom date. So we helped nature along by "planting" massive amounts of cut tulips in planters to resemble a spring garden effect. The White House electricians even rigged up heaters and special lighting to take the edge off of the chilly night air. It was a concerted effort to trick nature – all in the name of floral diplomacy.

In the Yellow Oval Room, where the small oval table overlooking the Truman Balcony was set with four place settings of Clinton presidential china and a bouquet of apricot "Juliet" garden roses, the space literally glowed in the early evening light. Against the backdrop of the soft yellow walls in the Yellow Oval Room, the pale, creamy yellow of the Clinton china was always a good choice. I created the apricot centerpiece in a gilded Tiffany vermeil bamboo basket, a lovely-proportioned container that always presented the flowers beautifully – just another example of Jackie Kennedy's exquisite taste and elegant style legacy. She had first selected these pieces over 50 years ago; I always marveled at their perfection. In addition to the centerpiece design, we designed additional bouquets in the same apricot palette for the coffee tables, mantels, and side tables to extend the French style and garden theme throughout the room.

An idea I introduced during my White House tenure was the "presentation bouquet"– a small hand-held bouquet of flowers that the First Lady gave to her guests at the end of a dinner or afternoon tea. My approach to this piece involved researching a guest's favorite colors and flowers to create a design that conveyed special meaning. At the appointed time, a butler would appear with the bouquet, displayed on a silver platter, wrapped in a coordinating silk ribbon bow with a handmade calligraphy gift tag, ready for the First Lady to present. Given Mrs. Obama's interest in making all guests feel welcome at the White House, the flowers were a personal touch, communicating her sentiments perfectly. Over the years, the use of the presentation bouquet expanded from official events to private outings. When Mrs. Obama ventured out to visit friends in the D.C. area, she often requested a little gift bouquet to take with her. This became a signature style statement for Mrs. Obama and created a very special and meaningful gift.

At the end of the evening with the Sarkozys, just as the guests made their way from the Yellow Oval Room, to the Center Hall and then to the Elevator vestibule that would take them back down to the North Portico and a waiting car, a White House butler picked up the Vermeil tray displaying a small bouquet of white flowers, gingerly handing the bouquet to the First Lady. The presentation bouquet honored Carla Bruni – a former Chanel model and current French recording artist – with a design of elegant all white flowers, variegated greens and ferns, wrapped with a dove gray silk bow: the Chanel Bouquet. The First Lady gave the bouquet to her guest as a symbol and gift of friendship – making a personal and memorable statement of floral diplomacy.

FRANCE STATE VISIT
PRESIDENT HOLLANDE

The February, 2014 state dinner with France, honoring President Hollande, was an historic event – the first official state visit between the U.S. and France in almost 20 years. The dinner featured a theme inspired by French impressionist paintings and Claude Monet's garden at Giverny. The floral color palette of violet and turquoise was carried out the in the table linens, china, glassware, candles, and tall vases of blooming spring branches. The iris (fleur de lys), the French national flower, was prominently featured, along with spring flowers and foliage that were American grown. This dinner represented the second time that American grown flowers were prominently incorporated in Obama State Dinner designs (the India State dinner was the first), which was roundly applauded by the American Cut Flower industry and the members of Congress representing them. The blending of floral elements and symbolism highlighted the shared history and long-standing friendship between the United States and France.

For floral inspiration, I drew on my background and training in Paris as well as on historic White House traditions. The goal was to create a collection of French-themed displays. For the Blue Room bouquet, the centerpiece of the State Floor decor, I designed an opulent mix of blue and purple flowers made in the French impressionist style. I wanted the piece to exude an overall feeling of lightness and movement, as well as a sense of freshness as if it had been made *en plein air* (outdoors) like an impressionist painting. My technique involved "painting" with flowers using an open and airy composition of materials, adding "brushstrokes" of color, blurred lines and contours to resemble a shimmering Impressionist display. This bouquet complemented a piece I made for the State Dining Room, a large bouquet of French lilacs, roses, lilies and orchids with jasmine and ivy that was created in the French garden style with free-flowing lines and vines emanating from a classical bouquet. We had to shuffle the furniture around a bit to fit the décor requirements. For example, the Old Family Dining room table went to the adjacent State Dining Room to become the presentation table for the floral display.

Then, the State Dining Room table travelled to the East Room where it displayed the Monroe Plateau in its full, spectacular glory. This time, we decorated the historic piece with an array of fuchsia flowers and blooming branches, sprinkling small vases of individual orchids and roses in and around the display. The mantels held vermeil urns filled with bouquets of Yves Piaget garden roses. In this magical setting, the guests mingled over cocktails and hors d'oeuvres before walking through the Blue Room and down the South Portico steps to the dinner tent on the South Lawn.

The flowers for the pre-state dinner reception in the private residence also carried out the French garden-style theme. Here, I took inspiration from President Hollande's hometown of Rouen, France, an idyllic town on the north coast of Normandy that was founded in the Middle Ages. The Jardin des Plantes de Rouen is a famous botanical garden with a notable collection of fuchsias, iris and roses – an inspiring place with sentimental meaning that I interpreted with mixed flowers and foliage in the Center Hall bouquet. Additional bouquets, including a trio of arrangements that symbolized the tripartite motto of France – Liberté, Égalité and Fraternité – created more opportunities for honoring the French guests.

Over 50 years ago, former First Lady Jacqueline Kennedy celebrated French floral art by weaving simple garden flowers and stylish embellishments, including fruits and flowering branches, into French bouquets that became part of her signature style and White House tradition. At this France state dinner, the goal was to integrate elements of French design and floral techniques in every aspect of the evening's décor. Using flowers, symbolism, colors, and historical pieces from the White House collection, we wove an integrated tapestry of individual designs that told the story of the longstanding friendship between the U.S. and France and honored the French president and his delegation. As President Hollande said in his toast to President Obama: "The United States of America and France are two great nations. What is expected of them is to keep a promise, a promise of freedom and the promise of progress, and also to keep a dream alive – that same dream made by Jefferson, Washington, Lafayette and the French revolutionaries – a dream to change the world. By uniting our forces, by uniting our talents, we will be able to keep the flame of hope alive."

Having studied French floral design in Paris for 15 years and experienced the beauty of that city, I was privileged and honored to create French floral design at the White House for these events, to honor the presidents of France, to make a presentation bouquet for the First Lady of France, and to continue the tradition of outstanding friendship and mutual respect that exists between our countries.

CAMP DAVID

Since 1942, Camp David, in Maryland's Catoctin Mountains, has served as a presidential retreat and official meeting place for all U.S. Presidents. Named after President Eisenhower's son, Camp David has been the site of some of the world's most historic diplomatic events. Over the years, the Obamas visited Camp David several times for official meetings with world leaders and private events such as the President's birthday. Located about two hours away by car (and a short helicopter ride via Marine One), Camp David is both a quiet and tranquil Presidential getaway – and a venue for high-level international affairs of state. Very few people ever have the opportunity to go there.

The White House is staffed by federal civilian workers while Camp David is run by the U.S. Navy. Whenever the President and First Lady made plans to visit Camp David, which could sometimes occur on very short notice, we put a design plan for flowers in place that had been agreed upon early on in the Obama Administration. The flowers were placed in all of the main cabins as well as any guest cabins that were occupied. The types of designs differed from my regular White House portfolio.

The Camp David arrangements were more casual and rustic, with flowers arranged in wooden baskets, terra cotta and clay pots. We often used woodlands elements – moss, ferns, and simple field flowers in these designs.

In May, 2012, President Obama hosted the G-8 summit at Camp David for key world leaders and their delegations. The two-day summit involved a series of diplomatic meetings (both bi-lateral and plenary sessions) as well as a complex schedule of meals, activities, and logistical arrangements along with extensive floral requirements. I worked closely with colleagues in the State Department to develop the floral template and timeline for the summit. The Protocol Office provided briefing notes on the color and flower preferences for each leader. Overall, I was responsible for creating close to 150 arrangements that would be used throughout the complex in meeting rooms, public spaces and private cabins.

As part of the planning process, I participated in a site visit to Camp David a couple of months before the actual summit.

As we navigated the narrow country roads on the way to Camp David, I sensed the increased altitude as my ears popped from the changing pressure. The winding road ran parallel to a river that was rushing with the spring runoff. The landscape features rolling woodland hills and wildflower fields that evoke a sense of rugged, untouched American wilderness. A hint of cool freshness was in the air that day in contrast to the warm, muggy conditions we left in Washington, D.C. There were several checkpoints once we entered the perimeter of the property. At one of the gates, we were asked to hand over all cell phones, cameras and other electronic devices. No photos were allowed.

We entered the final gate and displayed our White House credentials, which were double-checked against an arrival list. We parked near the main cabin where our Navy hosts met us and took us on a tour of the facilities starting with the main Laurel cabin that would host the principals for dinners and gatherings. The cabin resembled a modern conference space with a tall stone fireplace, expansive living room with comfortable leather furnishings in tones of rust, taupe and brown,

creating a calm and serene atmosphere. I made notes about flower placements – for side tables, coffee tables, and the grand piano in the corner. The adjacent dining room, which would host the meals with the principals, featured a large round table. Here, I planned to place a low, round centerpiece that would coordinate with the earthy colors in the dark-paneled room. I noticed a large 18th century open cupboard that contained a few pieces of yellow ocher pottery. I jotted down some additional notes about color and space, trying to remember as much as possible.

Next, we toured the meeting spaces – the conference rooms that would be set up for multi-lateral discussions and press conferences during the summit. The meeting rooms contained large rectangular tables that spanned the length of the room, surrounded by tall leather chairs. The flower requirements called for five long, low arrangements for each room that would create decoration in the space and disguise translation wires on the center of the table.

Our next stop on the tour was the individual cabins that were spread throughout the complex. To get there, we travelled by golf carts with our Navy escorts. These cabins would host the world leaders while they attended the summit. While the cabins varied in size and proximity to the main cabin (with the largest and closest cabins being most desirable), they were all well-appointed and comfortably furnished with bedrooms, adjoining sitting rooms, and small kitchenettes. Each cabin was slated to receive 2 or 3 arrangements to make the occupants feel at home. Again, I took notes about color schemes, placement and layouts. After the tour, we all met in the Laurel cabin to finalize logistical details with White House staff – including butlers and chefs as well as Camp David personnel and State Department staff.

Back at my desk, I created a spreadsheet and work plan that outlined the major milestones and timelines for carrying out the project. It involved mapping out a design plan for each cabin and meeting space based on my notes from the site visit and incorporating the detailed notes from the Protocol Office on flower requirements and preferences of each world leader. I also developed a plan for replacing key flowers as needed during the course of the 2-day event.

Once the design plan was in place, we ordered the containers for each piece: contemporary 'rustic chic' ceramic vases in various neutral shades of taupe, sage green, and robin's egg blue. Then I developed the flower recipes for each design, emphasizing domestically grown seasonal flowers. As we approached the date of the event, we launched a major operation in the flower shop – setting up tables outside for receiving and processing the flowers and organizing them by color, location and specific design project. Another team prepared the containers – cutting foam and inserting a base of greens. I led a design team that worked with me day and night to complete the arrangements. Upon completion, we moved them to a large refrigerated truck to transport the flowers to Camp David.

The day before the summit, an assistant and I were whisked away by a White House carpet van to Camp David where we personally placed all of the flowers, off-loading them from the truck and then onto golf carts that we used to deliver the bouquets, chauffeured by Navy personnel. The final piece I delivered was a large yellow bouquet for the dining table in the Laurel cabin. It would be the venue for the first official event of the summit, an informal dinner hosted by the President. When I created the piece, I thought of its symbolic placement in the center of the table of world leaders. Each person would experience the flowers in a unique way, based on their individual and cultural backgrounds – and perhaps based on their perspective as the leader of a nation. On a superficial level, the leaders might understand yellow as the color of friendship and a symbol of the spirit of the summit. But delving deeper, the flowers could mean something more personal to each person. President François Hollande might note the yellow iris in the bouquet – the national flower of France. German Chancellor Merkel might focus on the fact that yellow is her favorite color and recall that the White House honored her with yellow flowers two years before. Prime Minister Yoshihiko Noda of Japan, whose birthday would be celebrated at the dinner, could see the bouquet as the marker of a personal milestone. What is remarkable about flowers is their ability to evoke different memories for each participant and to make them feel comfortable in an otherwise foreign environment.

Meanwhile, back at the White House, Mrs. Obama engaged in her own diplomatic mission, inviting the spouses of G-8 leaders to tour the White House followed by a luncheon in the Blue Room prepared by celebrity chef Jose Andres. For this intimate event, the First Lady chose a cheerful color scheme of yellow spring flowers, the Clinton china and a bold-patterned yellow and cream linen with silver accents. After the luncheon, the First Lady presented each spouse with a personalized gift bag we prepared containing honey from the White House bees and seed packets from the White House garden. The gift was tied with co-ordinating ribbon and a hand-calligraphy card that contained a message of warm wishes from the First Lady.

Before leaving Camp David, I took a moment to look around, soaking up the ambiance of what would be another historic gathering. I felt very privileged to be one of the few people to have a chance to visit this special place and to contribute a multi-layered and personalized diplomatic floral backdrop for the meeting of the G-8 world leaders. It was floral diplomacy for a diplomatic event.

GOVERNORS' DINNER

Next to state dinners, the annual "Governors' Dinner" is the most elaborate and beautiful dinner that occurs at the White House. The event is held on the third Sunday in February when the weather is still wintry in Washington, D.C., but the promise of spring flowers and blooming branches, including the famous cherry blossoms is tantalizingly near. It is a chance for each state's top official to attend a glittery evening hosted by the President and First Lady, and – whether they are Democrats or Republicans – to enjoy an elegant evening in the intimate setting of the White House State Dining Room. It is a coveted invitation that brings politicians together across the political divide.

We started planning the Governors' Dinner soon after the holiday season each year. Mrs. Obama wanted to showcase the White House with elegant flowers and décor, a special menu and professional lighting. The first Governors' Dinner I planned was in 2010. That year, shortly after returning from the January Paris gift show that highlights new trends in décor and design, I presented several styles to the First Lady. The first option featured silvery gray linens with lavender flowers and the cobalt blue-rimmed Wilson and Roosevelt china services. A second alternative emphasized yellow and cream flowers, including daffodils, tulips and calla lilies, coordinating yellow and silver-patterned linens with the Clinton china, an homage to spring. The final option featured bold black and white graphic linens and the Reagan china with deep coral roses, orchids and hydrangea centerpieces presented in mirrored glass cubes. The First Lady chose the boldest option: the graphic and modern concept of black and white linens with a punch of glowing coral color that would be reflected via candlelight throughout the State Dining Room.

The night of the event, just before the guests arrived, the butlers lit the votive and taper candles that decorated the room, illuminating the entire space in a soft amber glow. The mirrored centerpiece containers captured the candlelight, amplifying the coral flowers, creating the illusion that they were floating on the table. With its distinctive orange-red border, the Reagan china was a perfect complement to the flowers and created a striking contrast on the black and white-patterned tablecloths. The décor was understated and chic, while introducing some modern design elements like mirrored cubes and Parisian-inspired bouquets. At the same time, the goal was to highlight the ambiance and historic collections of the White House – the architecture, furnishings, Reagan china, and vermeil collection. After all, this is what guests expect to experience and see when they attend a White House event.

When given a choice, the First Lady usually favored bright color combinations for official events rather than pastel or muted themes. So for the next Governors' Dinner in 2011, we added even more color to the event. The First Lady chose a bold and colorful presentation of vivid orange and fuchsia flowers in crisp white ceramic cubes placed on fuchsia, turquoise and orange-flocked linens – all in the same pattern but with different hues. I used coordinating bright shades of orange and fuchsia roses with mokara orchids for the centerpiece designs with accents of cattelaya orchids and trailing jasmine. We wrapped the jasmine around the crystal candlesticks and white candles, tying them off with additional orchids to resemble butterflies. In the professionally lit State Dining Room with apricot and rosy washes accenting the architectural details, the effect of the colors, candles and floating butterfly orchids was especially beautiful.

The following year, I created a set of new options for the décor based on current trends in the design world while also considering what works well in the State Dining Room. My process was to first develop an "inspiration board" of color palettes, linens, china, chair and table top options in a digital format. Without a budget for or access to graphics technology at the White House, I turned to volunteers for help. We created concepts and themes, color palettes and design elements that translated into concise and colorful digital presentations. It was the best way to show the overall ambiance and individual elements of a proposed design scheme. Based on feedback from colleagues in the First Lady's office, I could then create full prototypes and options for Mrs. Obama to review. In 2012, she chose a green "trellis garden" theme with celadon green patterned tablecloths on a silvery background, silver metallic garden chairs, bouquets alternating between lilac and green, and the Bush china – with its green trellis pattern – that tied together the whole look.

The White House Governors' Dinner typically coincides with the Academy awards – Hollywood's biggest night. In 2013, Mrs. Obama took a break from her evening to do a live broadcast from the White House to announce the "Best Picture" award which was broadcast around the world. The secrecy surrounding this live broadcast was unusually intense. Television crews with secure satellite technology arrived days in advance, setting up several levels of "fail-safe" transmission, repeatedly testing each system. The logistics surrounding the announcement of the winning film were also tightly controlled. At one point during the preparations, a member of the First Lady's communications team rushed into the flower shop. "Can we get 10 volunteers to the Diplomatic Room right now?" The volunteers stopped working and were instructed to leave their cell phones behind. I escorted them to the room where they were divided into groups. No one knew what was happening or was about to happen. Then, the First Lady arrived, smiling "Hey guys, how's it going?" It was the dress rehearsal for the live announcement and the flower shop volunteers served as stand-ins for the military personnel who would be there for the actual event. The idea called for the First Lady to mingle with each group and then come to the middle of the room to announce the big prize – the Oscar for "Best Picture of the Year." Most of the volunteers were star struck as they met the First Lady, except for one bold volunteer who asked: "what are you wearing tonight?" She laughed, grabbing his arm, saying it was "top secret." As she rehearsed her lines, Mrs. Obama announced a place-holder winner of best picture. The real winner would be kept under wraps until later that night. After the dinner, the First Lady made her way to the Diplomatic Room, where her announcement of Best Picture was beamed to millions of people around the world and went off without a hitch. The winner of the Academy Award? It was Argo. What was she wearing? A glittery gown from one of her favorite designers, Naeem Khan.

The 2014 Governors' dinner was an especially memorable one for me. The theme was "garden roses" and the State Dining Room décor featured opulent displays of roses in tall glass vases and the vermeil bamboo centerpieces. Rose and pink flowers were illuminated by special lighting that gave the room a rosy cast. After I finished the set-up for the dinner and sent the volunteers home, I went back to the flower shop to work on the next set of projects and events. Around 8:30 p.m. or so, a West Wing colleague rushed in to the flower shop, gesturing wildly, out of breath. "You need to come upstairs right now, the Governor of Washington wants to meet you." I protested a bit, saying that I wasn't dressed appropriately. But she was insistent, grabbing my hand and running with me as we made our way upstairs. Near the entrance of the State Dining Room, Washington Governor Inslee stood smiling with his wife. My colleague introduced us, noting that I was originally from Washington State as we compared notes about our roots in rural southwest Washington. The Governor grew up in the small town where my mother now lives, an amazing coincidence. "Listen, I have to tell you something," he said, leaning in. "Tonight we were seated at the head table with the President". He went on, "I asked him 'what will you miss most when you leave the White House in a couple of years?' Without missing a beat, he said, simply, 'the flowers.' The Governor said he thought that was wonderful, that I should feel proud, and that he was proud as a fellow Washingtonian. He asked if he could take a picture with me to post on his Twitter feed. I laughed, surprised by the Governor's aptitude with social media. Our visit ended when a social office staffer stepped in to usher the Governor and his wife to the East Room for the evening's entertainment. The flowers made a lasting impression on the guests that night – and apparently on the President – as reported by the Governor of my home state. It was an unforgettable night of floral diplomacy.

CONGRESSIONAL EVENTS

Over the past eight years, gridlock in Washington, D.C. intensified and the relationship between the Republican-controlled Congress and the White House was often tense and contentious. The traditional congressional events at the White House: the annual Congressional Holiday Ball, Congressional Spouses' Luncheon, and Congressional Picnic on the South Lawn were important opportunities for members of both parties to come together and interact in social settings at the White House, creating a brief respite from the bitter partisan divide. Flowers and décor always played an important role.

Congressional Ball.

The annual Congressional Ball is held in early December just as the holidays at the White House are ramping up with a full-scale onslaught of back-to-back parties, receptions, open houses and other events. It's an elegant evening honoring Members of Congress and their family members, a large and festive party for over 1,200 invited guests. The White House Office of Legislative Affairs, in conjunction with the Social Office and White House staff (florists, butlers, chefs, etc.), work together on the logistics and details for the event. Décor requirements include holiday-themed linens for the buffet and cabaret cocktail tables, coordinating cushion covers for the White House's gold ballroom chairs, and fresh flowers that are placed throughout the state room floors and on all of the tables. I proposed colors and concepts that coordinated with the overall holiday décor theme – usually classic and traditional combinations such as green and red or winter white with touches of silver and gold.

During these events, when the parties are in full swing, the President and First Lady descend the Grand Staircase to give a few welcome remarks in the Grand Foyer. It's fascinating to see guests, even Members of Congress, whip out their cell phones to capture the remarks, the glow of the screens adding additional illumination to the glittery holiday display. After the official welcome, the President and First Lady slip down to the Diplomatic Reception Room on the ground floor, which is turned into a photo studio and receiving line. The "photo ops" with the President and First Lady are highly organized and tightly scripted events. In order to move 1,200 people through the photo line within 2 ½ hours, visitors are given a color-coded scrap of paper upon arrival that tells them when to stand in line, with appointed times staggered in 15-minute intervals throughout the evening. The line snakes through the Lower Cross Hall, marked off by velvet rope and stanchions, with bars and buffet tables handy to keep guests in a jolly mood. The first stop is the Map Room, where guests are greeted by military aides who engage them in conversation and write down names and relationships on little cards. Visitors holding glasses or plates are encouraged to hand them to butlers, who are discreetly standing nearby. Purses, handbags and cameras are also collected and handed off to military aides – ostensibly to create a hands-free, clutter-free photo op, but also giving increased insurance that potential gift-givers or autograph-seekers are thwarted before they reach the First Couple. When they enter the side door of the Diplomatic room, a photographic screen blocks off the view of the fireplace area where the principals are standing. But they can hear the President's distinctive voice and

see the flash of the camera, pulsating strobe-like in the room. As Members of Congress snake around the oval-shaped room, they eventually come within close proximity and eyesight of the President and Mrs. Obama. A military aide appears just as the guests approach the principals to make the formal introduction. After a few seconds of small talk, the individual couple (or group) lines up for the official photo, captured by the White House photographer. There is but a moment to interact with them. Some guests may take the opportunity to make a point, offer a clever remark or even give unsolicited advice to the President. Within a minute, the military aide is there to gently (but firmly) escort the group into the China Room where guests can gather their belongings. The photo is sent to the Member a month or two after the holidays, a highly coveted memento of a beautiful and enjoyable evening. It's a tradition that no matter how divisive or contentious things are in Washington, during the Congressional holiday party at the White House, the allure of a smiling photo with the President and First Lady trumps politics – at least for that fleeting moment. The backdrop is the gaily decorated mantel of the Diplomatic Room fireplace with the famous portrait of George Washington gazing down on the guests. One can just imagine George being amused at the odd pairings of political adversaries posing below him, permanently captured with frozen smiles for posterity.

Congressional Spouses' Luncheon.

Each year, the First Lady hosts a luncheon for congressional spouses at the White House. Since it's a relatively small event with only about 60 people in attendance, it can be held in an intimate setting like the Blue Room. In 2010, a few months into my tenure as Chief Floral Designer, I selected décor for the luncheon, including pink and peach linens, china and flowers with a spring ladies' luncheon theme. (Although there are Congressional spouses who are men, none were able to attend that event). Behind my computer, a small cabinet held samples of the Presidential china that could be used for White House events. For this luncheon with a pink and peach floral scheme, I selected the Lyndon B. Johnson china from the cabinet – a pastel wild-flower-patterned design which was inspired by Lady Bird's highway beautification and conservation initiatives in the 1960s. The plates feature wildflowers from every state – an ideal motif for a congressional event with attendees from across the country. It coordinated perfectly with the flowers and linens. Unbeknownst to me, however, the entire set of Johnson china had been banished to the White House warehouse months before. Some early White House staff

Spouses' Luncheon, the Johnson china with its lovely story of wildflowers representing the various states became a topic of conversation. Several guests lifted up the china to look at the maker, admiring it, noting that they had never seen it before. On their way out, they congratulated the junior social office staffer on his unconventional and clever choice of Presidential china for the event. Seeing me standing nearby, he winked and flashed a quick thumbs up. Floral diplomacy – it's always a team effort.

White House South Lawn events.

The South Lawn of the White House is often called "the nation's backyard." It is an ideal site for large celebrations ranging from Halloween and the Easter Egg Roll to 4th of July and state arrival ceremonies and even meetings with the Pope. With a spectacular view of the South Portico of the White House and the Washington Monument below, the grounds can accommodate thousands of people for picnics and receptions, "Let's Move" exercise routines led by the First Lady, kitchen garden harvests and countless other activities. But it's also the First Family's back yard, a place where the First Dogs run and play, where the President walks the grounds with key advisors and has a chance to grab a bit of fresh air inside "the bubble" of White House life. It's a place where the Obamas enjoyed family barbecues and pool parties over the years just like a regular American family – that happens to live at the nation's most famous address. When planning an outdoor event, the elements play a critical role. In good weather, the White House South Lawn is a spectacular place. However, the threat of inclement weather always lurks as potential possibility, imperiling plans, forcing last minute changes and creative solutions to ward off décor disasters. Depending upon the time of year, we could face gale force winds, hurricanes, sweltering heat, and even swarming White House bees. Over the years, we confronted all of the above.

members and design advisors apparently thought that the set was outdated and old-fashioned, and they did not envision it ever being used in the Obama White House. However, after seeing the china and how it complemented the décor scheme (and carried out the message of wildflowers across America) I felt confident that it was the correct choice for this event. After I recommended it, a junior social office staffer nervously called his boss, the social secretary, who was boarding a flight for Chicago. "Is it alright to use the Johnson china?" he asked. When he explained that the setting actually looked quite nice and then followed up via e-mail with photographic proof, she approved the concept and said we should go ahead with the plan. The next step was to reclaim the china from the off-site warehouse. Although the curators grumbled about having to retrieve and unpack the 200+ place settings, we brought the Johnson china back into the White House where it was used often during the Obama years. At the Congressional

Congressional picnics.

The Congressional Picnic is an annual event for the 535 Members of Congress and their families, a bi-partisan picnic with 2,000 or so people in attendance. The décor theme always revolves around an Americana theme: a cowboy barbecue, state fairs, baseball, etc. In partisan Washington where the political rhetoric is often heated and divided, the picnic represents a rare opportunity for a relaxed family evening around a unifying theme of celebrating American life.

One year, the theme was "Boots and Barbecue" – a southern style barbecue with a cowboy theme. It was scheduled for mid-June on the South Lawn. Even though it was a nice day with the temperature hovering in the low 80s, there was a slight breeze blowing that made the air temperature seem slightly cooler. It was perfect weather. We placed hundreds of little wildflowers bouquets displayed in mason jars on the red and white checked picnic tables. Just as we were finishing up and heading back to the flower shop to clean up, I received word that there was a crisis on the South Lawn – a "flower emergency" -- that required my immediate attention.

I raced outside, staring at the scene that was unfolding in front of me. In just a few minutes, the winds had picked up, turning the south grounds into a whistling wind tunnel of surprisingly brisk summer breezes. The hundreds of mason jar arrangements that we had just carefully placed on the picnic tables, top heavy with wildflowers, were toppling over like dominoes, spilling water on the linens, and then tumbling to the ground. With less than an hour to go to until the guests arrived, we needed to come up with a solution very fast. Thinking on her feet, a clever volunteer suggested placing the mason jars in clear glass cubes – this would still give the rustic effect of mason jars while adding the stability of the cube to prevent the flowers from falling over. The problem with this brilliant solution? We had hundreds of glass cubes on site, but they had just been painstakingly wrapped with red, white and blue ribbon in preparation for the upcoming 4th July celebration. Now the work had to be undone – quickly – in order to resolve the wind-blown flower crisis. Everyone jumped in to unwrap the vases, no one complained, and the situation was averted. Despite the unexpected weather challenge, bi-partisan political and floral diplomacy carried on that evening.

A different kind of scenario unfolded at another Congressional Picnic event. That year, the theme was "American Country" featuring food stations from different regions around the country – Pacific Northwest salmon, southern barbecue, Chicago pizza, Maryland crab, and other delights. The décor scheme was simple but elegant: burlap linen table cloths topped by large planters of colorful petunias in terra cotta pots. After completing the set-up, I took one last look and made a final walk through the décor set-up to ensure that the plants were watered and the linens were secured. Then I went back to the flower shop to continue work on the weekly portfolio and the week's upcoming events. About a half hour into the event, I received an unusual call: apparently the burlap linens were giving off static electricity and shocking the guests. I was summoned to the South Lawn to assess the situation and devise a solution. According to the chefs and butlers, when guests left the cotton candy station with their freshly made confection, they returned to their seats only to be jolted with electricity after touching the burlap fabric. With the bizarre drama quickly escalating, I tried to recall lessons from my high school science class. It appeared that the metal spoon used to stir the cotton candy served as a conductor, creating an imbalance of electrical charges on the surface of the fabric. The solution? Water and fabric softener sheets. The water would increase the humidity while the fabric softener would neutralize the build-up of static electricity. I ran back to the White House, grabbed a spray bottle and a roll of "Bounce" sheets from the laundry team, discreetly spraying the tables and slipping a Bounce sheet under the burlap as guests went to the buffet table. My take-away from that experience: always expect the unexpected when implementing outdoor White House events.

Not all of the congressional picnic events ended with a décor or flower challenge. The 2014 congressional picnic, featuring an all-American baseball theme (America's favorite past-time) went off without a hitch, a perfect blend of classic Americana décor (baseball topiary centerpieces in wheat grass containers), food (hot dogs) and venue (the White House South Lawn) on a brilliant fall day – to create a fun evening of political diplomacy with Members of Congress and families. My favorite memory of the event was looking out the Diplomatic Room door at the South Portico when the party was in full swing. Children were laughing and playing with large 4 ft. round rubber beach balls (painted to resemble giant baseballs) that I had ordered as decorative props, kicking and throwing them to each other on the grounds, the giant balls floating and bouncing in slow motion as the sun set against the backdrop of the Washington monument. It was a timeless scene of fun and frivolity – and classic floral diplomacy.

The annual 4th of July Independence Day celebration on the White House South Lawn is a highlight of the year, featuring classic American barbecue, country music, and patriotic décor. The theme is unabashedly all-American. Vintage bunting is hung from the Truman balcony, the tables are dressed in red, white and blue and a military band decorated in revolutionary garb marches back and forth across the grounds. The event is a three-part affair: in the late afternoon, active military members and their families are invited to join the President and First Lady for a barbecue and picnic. Later, in the early evening, a few thousand additional guests, including White House staff members and their families, are invited to view the fireworks display from the best spot in the city – the White House grounds. Once the main party is underway and the President has made his formal remarks, the First Couple escapes to the adjacent pool area near the Oval Office. Here, a private party is held for Obama friends and family members that has a birthday theme in honor of Malia, their oldest daughter who was born on the 4th of July. After a typical July 4th meal – hamburgers, hot dogs and all of the accompaniments – the family retires to the Solarium on the third floor of the residence where they can exit on to the roof for a prime view of the fireworks.

For the flower shop, it means planning décor and flowers for three different events. Given the scope of the project, involving over 100 centerpieces and 30 cocktail arrangements on the South Lawn, additional décor for the pool party and private residence, I started working on our plans months in advance. A key consideration for 4th of July is the weather – the temperature is always at least 90 degrees and sometimes soars to over 100. With high humidity and long hours outside in the direct sun, it is a challenge to keep flowers fresh and wilt-free throughout the event. Over the years, I experimented with various strategies. One year, we used small pots of geraniums as centerpiece displays, watering them frequently throughout the day of the event. Another year, I opted for a flower-free approach: 3-tiered cake-stand centerpieces made from simple paper plates that displayed fruit and lollipop-style topiaries. These designs were whimsical and festive – and they didn't wilt. It was possible to use flowers, however, by employing a few key strategies. First, the selection of hardy, long-lasting flowers was key. Second, a water source is required to keep the flowers hydrated. One of my favorite designs involved creating cubes of red, white and blue flowers featuring bases made of alternating stripes of red and white carnations topped with fluffy local blue hydrangea. It was patriotic and chic all at the same time.

One of the most memorable 4th of July celebrations I worked on was in 2014. We made red, white and blue bouquets in disposable containers with the idea that guests would take them at the end of the evening as souvenirs. After a long day in the sun, the flowers have little life left in them and must be disposed of at the end of the evening. Additional party favors included chair seat medallions – decorations featuring an image of the White House that we hung on the back of the chairs with ribbon. That year, after completing all of the décor requirements and set ups, I took a break and joined my husband at the party. As a White House employee, it was always an honor to attend the fireworks and concert portion of the event, no matter how exhausted I was from the long day. We sat down at a table with several other people who were already there as part of the military portion of the event. To my right was a PhD psychologist who volunteers at Walter Reed Army Hospital helping the most severely injured soldiers – the ones who have lost limbs, suffered traumatic brain injuries, and who face unfathomable challenges and hardships. She told us how she supports them, listens to their stories, and tries to give them hope to reclaim their lives. She said that she was taking pictures and making notes of the White House 4th of July experience so that she could share it with her soldiers who were too sick and injured to leave their hospital beds. I was incredibly impressed and moved by her story of dedication to these injured troops.

To my immediate left was an army sergeant and his wife. He was also from Walter Reed. And he had a heartbreaking story. After serving nine deployments, including three to Iraq and one to Afghanistan, he returned to his home in North Carolina. There, in his own front yard, a drunk driver hit him in broad daylight, severing both of his legs. For the last two years, the soldier had been in rehabilitation at Walter Reed, learning to walk again and to use prosthetic legs. His wife spoke frankly about the struggles they face every day – the feelings of depression and despair, the fear of what the future holds, the difficulty of being away from home for so long. And, yet they were there on the White House lawn with the Commander in Chief on the most significant day honoring freedom and the American ideal. And they felt honored to be there. Harboring no bitterness or self-pity, the couple truly exemplified the best of the American spirit.

After the fireworks, I knew what I would do. I turned to the wife and explained my position at the White House. I said that I would be honored if she took one of my centerpieces as a way to commemorate the couple's White House experience and to serve as a symbol of a nation's appreciation for their service and sacrifice – as well as my personal gratitude for having the opportunity to meet them and hear their inspiring story of strength and perseverance. She became emotional, saying 'Thank you, Miss Laura, I'll never forget this'. I watched as the sergeant stood up on his prosthetic legs and slowly and deliberately made his way towards the exit, his wife helping him along, with the flowers in hand.

I also offered flowers to the dedicated volunteer from Walter Reed. She was thrilled, saying that she would take the flowers to the hospital the very next day so that her soldiers could see them while she recounted all of the stories from the event. The doctor thanked me profusely for this small gesture, saying it would mean so much to her patients. As we all made our way to the exit, I lost sight of the people from our table as they merged in to a moving throng of humanity. Then I happened to look over to the side of the road and saw both of my Walter Reed tablemates being stopped by a Secret Service agent. He was telling them to put the flowers down. There in the shadows, I could see a pile of bedraggled centerpieces growing bigger as other guests were asked to relinquish their floral souvenirs. I recognized the agent and ran up to him. 'No, no, these flowers are meant to be given away,' I said. He smiled and said, 'Oh, OK, you would know.' My Walter Reed friends smiled in relief and retrieved their 4th of July bouquets. At the White House venue on that patriotic day, the flowers represented more than table decorations. They symbolized the strength and resilience of the human spirit – and I was honored and humbled to have been a part of this experience.

HALLOWEEN

Another official South Lawn event where weather plays a crucial role is the annual Halloween party for 5,000 school children and military family members. The White House Halloween is always held on the actual day, October 31, which means the weather can be dicey. Over the years, it ranged from pleasant and balmy to dreary and cold, with snow falling one year as the costumed trick-or-treaters entered the White House gates, covering them and the autumn-themed decorations with a wintry blast. In 2012, the White House Halloween was cancelled in the wake of Hurricane Sandy which devastated the Northeast and caused high winds and rainy conditions in Washington, D.C. But usually the strategy is to soldier on despite challenging weather conditions.

Our preparations for Halloween started months in advance given the huge size of the event with large-scale decorations featured throughout the South Lawn, at the South Portico, and on the southern façade of the White House, including the Blue Room and Truman balconies. My typical starting point was an inspiration board that featured ideas and design elements that conveyed a specific theme – whether it was "Classic Halloween," "Autumn Splendor," or "Modern Halloween." The color scheme is obvious – black, white and orange – perhaps with accents of silver or gold. But depending upon which elements are emphasized (e.g., black cats, spiders, and witches vs. pumpkins, hay bales and scarecrows), it's possible to change the ambiance and mood of the Halloween event – tilting it towards an Autumn seasonal theme or emphasizing more traditional Halloween decor. The only strict rule of thumb was to avoid overtly scary images such as gory or violent scenes in order to keep the tone family-friendly. The inspiration board provided a game plan and template for moving forward with specific project ideas.

Given the endless supply of motivated volunteers who were eager to help me with White House events, we could contemplate very ambitious projects for Halloween. This included lining the entire drive with hundreds of hand-carved pumpkins, making 10 ft. wreaths out of thousands of fall leaves, crafting huge garlands made from orange and black plastic sheeting, creating giant pumpkin topiaries and other very labor-intensive projects. The Bo and Sunny replicas that we made for our annual holiday display were brought up from the "dog pen" at the warehouse and dressed up for Halloween. A couple of clever costumes stand out. One year, a volunteer with a circus background took "classic" Bo (made from 40,000 twisted black and white pipe cleaners) on a secret mission to his studio in Baltimore for the measuring of a costume with a pirate theme. He created a pirate costume consisting of a tri-cornered hat and billowy striped breeches tied with a colorful sash. The finishing pirate touches included the requisite eye-patch and a parrot to sit on Bo's shoulder, accessorized with a treasure chest full of dog bones. Within 48 hours, the costumer was back with Bo festooned as a pirate for his White House Halloween debut. Standing there at the North Portico during the official trick-or-treating event, Pirate Bo delighted guests, young and old alike.

Another year, we expanded on the circus theme when Sunny, Bo's younger sister joined the scene (and the warehouse dog-pen). This time, volunteers created Bo and Sunny as clown jesters, complete with pompom hats and elaborate clown costumes. They were featured as part of a children's "Bo and Sunny Halloween Circus" where jugglers and acrobats performed near the adorable jester-dressed dogs. As the guests meandered up the south drive, which glowed with hundreds of LED-illuminated pumpkins and aerial acrobats performing overhead, they stopped at the South Portico where the President and First Lady hand out treats, and then continued on the drive that eventually leads them out the White House gates.

On a couple of occasions, the White House Halloween occurred indoors where the President and First Lady hosted smaller, but festive events for military children and families. In 2009, with help from Disney and Hollywood producers, we transformed the State Dining Room into the movie set for "Alice in Wonderland" complete with a serpentine table set for the Mad Hatter's tea. To decorate the space, the Hollywood team asked me to create creepy bouquets of dark red roses. That evening, while thousands of trick-or-treaters came to the North Portico for treats, a much smaller group of invited guests met Actor Johnny Depp in costume at the Mad Hatter's tea party, along with characters from Star Wars, who roamed the state floor. The following year, decorations included a giant bat mobile suspended from the North Portico, stacks of pumpkins and a garland made of fall leaves and gourds surrounding the door. After the White House treats were handed out to trick-or-treaters, the President and First Lady again invited a group of military families inside for a party and concert in the East Room. For the large buffet decorations, we created topiaries made of tall branches teeming with black crows. The cocktail tables featured small black cubes arranged with green apples that were wrapped in various patterns of black ribbons. We filled the vermeil urns on the East Room mantel with armfuls of dead flowers to carry out the haunted house theme. During the final walk through before the event, the social secretary, upon seeing the dead flowers that she had requested, joked "Laura, you really need to up your game." All in the spirit of floral diplomacy.

THE WHITE HOUSE
POLICY THEMES

LET'S MOVE

The First Lady's 'Let's Move' initiative provided some of the best inspiration for creative displays of White House floral diplomacy during my tenure. For events and every day arrangements, I often used fruit and vegetables in designs to support her priority of promoting kids' exercise and healthy eating. From holiday work and garden planting events to sporting themes and everyday arrangements, fruits and vegetables became a symbol of Let's Move – and White House style.

IDEA APPLE

For a 'Let's Move' party on the South Lawn for 1,000 educators, including cafeteria professionals, nutrition directors and school principals In October, 2011, we created a giant apple out of recycled faux apples from the White House collection and the Korea State dinner that was held a few days before. The apple is an iconic emblem of learning and a healthy lifestyle; it's also a perfect symbol for the Let's Move initiative. The apple became the motif for the educational event's décor and table decorations. Creating the giant apple was a team effort: the carpenters first carved the base of the apple out of a foam block, shaping it to resemble an apple form. Then volunteers covered the base with re-purposed faux apples from the White House collection. To make the apple appear as realistic as possible, we marked out patterns of gradations on the form using real apples as models. The 'stem' of the apple was a large tree branch from the White House grounds. To create an interactive design, we carved out a hole in the center of the apple to serve as a receptacle for ideas – on how to increase kids' healthy habits at school – that guests could drop inside. As guests enjoyed apple snacks, drank apple juice and dropped their creative suggestions into the giant apple made from re-purposed materials, the symbolism was obvious: education, Let's Move, and floral diplomacy on the South Lawn.

OVAL OFFICE APPLES.

Another place that apples took on special significance in the Obama White House was the Oval Office. During the George W. Bush Administration, a bowl of orange roses was the preferred decorative arrangement for the coffee table in the Oval Office. The florists provided this arrangement – one recipe using the same flowers – every day for eight years. After President Obama was inaugurated in 2009, he started a new tradition. The President changed the flower arrangement to a bowl of apples that became his signature decoration over the years. Whether it is art or furnishings or accessories, any décor in the Oval Office is subject to media scrutiny. For example, the placement of apples as decoration in the Oval Office made a strong statement of support for the First Lady's Let's Move Initiative. She also kept a comparable bowl of apples in her East Wing office. Yet the Oval Office apples seemed to embody meaning that went beyond Let's Move to symbolize a modern, fresh approach to policy and governing. The apples became a signature motif of the Obama Oval Office, a prominent feature in the most important office in the world. In addition to providing decoration and symbolism, they served a practical purpose, too. Throughout the day, staff and visitors were encouraged to eat the apples instead of junk food as a healthy snack alternative.

Behind the scenes, the flower shop team kept the apple bowls filled, ordering boxes of gala apples from Yakima, Washington. After trying a couple of different varieties, we learned that the gala apples were the Presidential apple of choice for both taste and appearance. Each day, around 7 a.m., a flower shop staff member would head to the Oval Office with apples and a watering can, replacing apples so that there was always a full bowl. The apples have been a constant in the Oval Office for the past 7 $\frac{1}{2}$ years. Except for one time. During the federal budget sequester in 2013 which forced the government to shut down for over two weeks, the bowl of apples was slowly depleted. Except for a very few White House staff who kept the White House open during that period, most of us were told to stay home. With no one there to replenish the apples, they became a marker of the sequester and passing time. By the end of the shutdown, only a few lonely apples were left in the Oval Office as recorded in official photographs and news coverage during that time. Floral (and apple) diplomacy were on hold until the budget impasse was over.

VEGGIE TORCH.

Every two years, the world comes together to celebrate Olympic athletes who represent the pinnacle of athletic achievement and the pursuit of excellence. Other than the Olympic rings, the most iconic symbol of the Olympics is the torch – the ceremonial flame that travels throughout the host country carried by prominent citizens, with the honor of the final leg of the journey given to a beloved athlete who exemplifies the Olympic ideals. As the runner scales the steps to light the Olympic cauldron that signifies the beginning of the Olympic Games, we are all inspired to embrace the Olympic spirit. The Olympics are the premier example of athletic diplomacy.

Every President maintains the long-standing tradition of inviting U.S. Olympians to the White House to be recognized for their achievements. The athletes are national heroes and a trip to the White House allows their victories to be celebrated on a national stage. I remember when the 'Fierce Five' women's gymnastics team came to the White House after their gold-medal winning performance at the 2012 London Olympics. They visited us in the flower shop where they sent excitable tweets from the cooler. From there, they took a tour of the state floors ending up in the Oval Office for a meet and greet with President Obama. Sixteen-year-old gymnast McKayla Maroney, who famously scowled after learning that she had earned a silver medal in the individual vault final, was surprised to learn that the President knew about her facial expression that became an international viral sensation. 'I want to talk to you for a minute about that face,' he said, continuing, 'It's one that I make at least once a day.' It was a light-hearted moment in the Oval Office: the Olympic gymnast making her famous 'unimpressed' face with the President displaying an impressive impression of the 'unimpressed' look alongside her. The moment was captured in an iconic photo that also went viral.

When we learned that the 2014 U.S. Winter Olympic and para-Olympic teams would visit the White House, it was exciting news. The teams had triumphed in Sotsji, Russia, with electrifying performances and uplifting stories of triumph and perseverance. The First Lady's office asked me to create a stylized Olympic torch for the event, a prop that would combine the symbolism of the Olympics with the Let's Move tenets of exercise and healthy eating. As soon as I received the request, I knew exactly what to do. I envisioned a torch made of vegetables with carrot and gloriosa lily flames emerging from an artichoke base, wrapped with a garland of bundled green beans. The athletes could carry the 'torch' (an iconic symbol of the Olympic games) into the White House (the nation's most iconic address) where it would take on even additional meaning, rendered in vegetables, as a symbol of the First Lady's signature health initiative. In addition to the veggie torch, I made ten 'victory' bouquets out of cabbages, Brussels sprouts and herbs – similar to the small bouquets that medal-winning athletes are handed as they ascend the Olympic podium. These bouquets served as additional props for the athletes, and, as symbols of victory and healthy eating, they provided further reinforcement of the overall theme, connecting the visual aesthetic with the policy message.

Over 200 athletes were invited to converge on the South Lawn for an Olympic-style welcoming ceremony at the White House. To create an Olympics-like atmosphere, there was a 'sportscaster' (the Director of Let's Move) who emceed the gathering and interviewed athletes about their favorite foods and how they fueled up for peak performance. The event was broadcast live on the White House web site. The athletes arrived at the White House on a beautiful early spring day – a postcard picture-perfect scene of pink blossoms, tulips and daffodils blooming on the South Grounds. As the Olympians marched in, led by Bo and Sunny, the First Family's friendly and popular Portuguese water dogs, they were bursting with energy, laughing and chatting with their teammates, jumping and cart-wheeling across the lawn. Julie Chu, a member of the U.S. hockey team, held aloft an Olympic-style flag with 'Let's Move' emblazoned on it. Gold medal-winning skier Michaela Schiffrin, the youngest athlete to ever win the giant slalom, was given the honor of carrying the veggie torch with carrot flames. Additional athletes carried the victory bouquets. All of the athletes seemed to understand intuitively the symbolic significance of their special veggie props: they spoke passionately about the connection between healthy eating and performance, referencing the victory bouquets and veggie torch during their interviews, posing for pictures with them, and holding them high. The convergence of Olympic and White House symbolism with veggie floral designs created an unexpected magical moment that resonated with people across the country. It conveyed both the essence of the inspiring Olympic ideal and the First Lady's health program in an exciting way.

KIDS' STATE DINNERS.

In 2012, Mrs. Obama launched the idea of a 'Kids' State Dinner', an annual gathering of children from across the country who enter a healthy eating recipe contest to compete for an invitation to the White House – a special luncheon with all of the pomp and circumstance of an official state dinner. The entries are innovative and sophisticated with clever names like 'Barack-amole' and 'Mic-Kale Obama Slaw'. The common denominator is the requirement that the recipes feature healthy ingredients that support the First Lady's Let's Move agenda. The students submit their original recipes for consideration that are judged by a panel of experts, including White House chefs.

The décor for these kids' luncheons is always fun and colorful, featuring centerpieces made of fruits and vegetables, stage backdrops of fruit, flower and veggie topiaries that create a lighthearted and energetic feeling in the East Room – which is usually a formal and serious space. My favorite decorations were always the large topiary displays that decorated the stage. These were the backdrops for the event that was hosted by the First Lady with a cameo appearance by the President. For these designs, the goal was to create drama and impact with clean lines of color and classical topiary shapes. One year the theme was citrus fruits. We incorporated everything from lemons and limes to oranges and grapefruits to create multi-colored designs that were placed on pedestals throughout the stage. These pieces coordinated with centerpieces made of flowers and vegetables – and even with the First Lady's dress that she wore to the event. Another year, we expanded on the fresh topiary theme, creating an entire backdrop of vegetable, fruit and flower arrangements designed to resemble a country farm stand display. For these pieces, I ordered everything that was in season at the local farmer's markets – thus carrying out a sub-theme of locally American grown and harvested materials. Cherries, carrots, squash, green beans, sunflowers, green apples and red apples were all part of the display.

In addition to the pieces we made for the East Room event, I often created coordinating designs for the State Floor rooms. The Kids' State Dinner program mirrored official State Dinners with announcements of guest arrivals, a receiving line in the Blue Room, and post-meal entertainment. Kids (with their escorts) even followed the same route as an official State Dinner, arrived at the East Entrance and then were guided upstairs to a pre-luncheon reception in the Grand Foyer. Instead of a cocktail hour, however, the bar was set up as a juice bar with kid-friendly options for the young guests. Here, the decorations were designed to tie into the Let's Move theme – with additional topiaries of fruit, including blueberry, strawberry and raspberry designs.

In the Blue Room, I replaced the typical garden style floral arrangements with vegetable and flower designs: squash and zucchini vases bursting with whimsical wildflower bouquets. For the Red Room, I created vases out of purple pearl onions and purple cabbage topped by red zinnias and dahlias. In many ways, the décor for a Kids' State Dinner was as elaborate as any 'real' official event – utilizing fresh elements from the garden, farmers' market and grocery aisle to create colorful and lively décor.

GARDEN HARVEST EVENTS.

Each year like clockwork in the fall and spring, the First Lady hosts a garden planting event with school children to promote her Let's Move initiative. Many of the school children come from local inner city schools; it is usually their first-time visit to the White House. In the spring, the event involves planting seeds and sowing beds, while the fall event includes harvesting the garden's bounty. The event always captures the interest of the press since Mrs. Obama herself dons gloves, happily tilling the earth alongside the school children. When they finish their work, the group is invited to sit down at gaily bedecked, red and white checked picnic tables to nosh on healthy snacks with the First Lady. Our decorations for these events always carried out the healthy eating theme and a casual, lighthearted floral scheme: flowers and vegetables arranged in cabbage vases, bowls of apples that also doubled as a snacking option, cheerful sunflower and tomato bouquets. Through these images, powerful messages were conveyed: the symbolism of nature and the changing seasons, of planting and harvesting, and sharing a table together. The event forged a solid link between healthy lifestyle and healthy eating, the activity and work (planting and harvesting) and the enjoyment of the results. One year, as the South Lawn was deluged by rain from a powerful spring storm, we moved the event inside to the State Dining Room. Here, the tables were set with simple bouquets of giant purple cabbages – one head per vase – the swirling leaves in tones of green, gray and lilac – adding just enough color and pattern to create a natural display. Cabbage and kale were woven into the menu as well that day, an idea that made vegetables and healthy eating top of mind – both on the plate and in the decorations.

JOINING FORCES

MOTHER'S DAY TEA
WITH PRINCE HARRY.

On Mother's Day 2013, the White House held its annual Mother's Day tea, hosted by the First Lady and Dr. Jill Biden, to honor military families and mothers of U.S. service personnel. The program always features an elegant high tea in the East Room and a temporary craft room that is set up in the State Dining Room. Here, the youngest guests – the children of military personnel – create special gifts and cards to present to their moms, led by the White House florists and chefs. Mrs. Obama and Dr. Biden stop by and visit each craft station, greeting the children and assisting them with their projects. The Obama family dogs, Bo and Sunny, often make a surprise visit to the tea as well, much to the delight of the children. This is always a favorite White House event.

My idea that year was to create a 'flower stand' for kids. The concept involved having the children select flowers for their bouquets from a colorful display that they would then finish off with rose petal wraps and ribbon bows. With over 60 children scheduled to participate and less than ½ hour to complete the bouquets, the bouquet-making operation needed to be fully staffed and organized with assembly line precision. Several of my favorite volunteers signed up to help me that day.

A few days prior to the Mother's Day tea, excitement was building over the prospect of a 'very special guest' who would be in attendance. The identity of the mystery guest was such a closely guarded secret that I didn't know who it was until the actual day of the event. When I told my volunteers that Prince Harry would be joining us to make Mother's Day bouquets, they nearly fainted at the prospect of having a chance to meet him. That afternoon, as we put together simple garden bouquets with the children, we were rendered somewhat star-struck as the adorable Prince with the mischievous grin made his way towards our table. In his distinctive British accent, familiar to millions around the world, he greeted us. 'Hello ladies,' he said, smiling, 'are we making bouquets today?' As one might expect from a young man who had been in the public eye all of his life, he was very engaging and charming. When I asked if he wanted to make a bouquet himself, he laughed, saying that he was 'all thumbs in that department.' But he noted that his entire family appreciated flowers and gardens. His father, Prince Charles, of course, is particularly noted for his love of horticulture and active participation in global conservation efforts. Prince Harry listened keenly as we demonstrated a condensed version of the garden style technique. He knelt down at the kids' eye level to admire their choice of flowers and colors. He was such a natural with the children and seemed to really enjoy himself.

Seeing the joy on the faces of the children working so hard on their bouquets with Prince Harry – and also on the faces of their moms when they received them – was a wonderful moment of White House magic. The reaction of my team of volunteers was equally rewarding. Three of the young women who worked with me that day have since become new mothers. Each year since the White House event, they've contacted me to reminisce about the experience. Their personal celebration of Mother's Day will always be intertwined with the memories of that special day. As Prince Harry stood by us at the bouquet-making station on this Mother's Day event, I couldn't help but recall the heart-wrenching scene at his mother's funeral, the funeral of Princess Diana, when he was only 10 years old. Who could forget the image of the young red-haired boy walking solemnly behind his mother's casket? One of the most iconic and powerful images of that tragic day was represented by the small bouquet of white roses on her casket and a card from her youngest son, addressed simply 'Mummy'. Recently, Prince Harry said in an interview that he regrets not sharing the pain of his personal loss over the years, noting that talking about his mother could have possibly helped others cope with their own grief and loss. Perhaps his thoughts were with her on Mother's Day as he inspired the children to create beautiful bouquets for their own mums. At the White House that day, he served as a perfect 'flower ambassador' for inspiring personal and heart-felt floral diplomacy.

PRESIDENTIAL WREATHS

Memorial Day is an important day at the White House; it's a day filled with patriotism and floral symbolism, solemn ceremonies and official remembrances of the nation's fallen war heroes. The President and First Lady host an annual White House breakfast for Gold Star families – those who have lost a loved one in service to our country – before taking a short motorcade ride to Arlington Cemetery to lay a Presidential wreath at the Tomb of the Unknown Soldier. An annual Memorial Day ritual for the White House flower shop team is the creation of the patriotic red, white and blue memorial wreath that the President places at Arlington Cemetery – as well as six additional wreaths that are laid at other war memorials in Washington, D.C. The wreaths are made according to a precise military recipe: a large base of mixed greens is covered in red and white carnations and blue iris and coordinating striped bow, attached to a simple white wreath stand. There is no room for any creative interpretation; the wreaths must be made exactly the same way with the same materials each year for every administration.

The process for creating these wreaths is highly organized with a specific timeline and project plan. A few weeks before Memorial Day, I checked to make sure that we had enough wreath forms and stands on hand along with the necessary wreath-making supplies (including bind-wire, wood picks, ribbon, Presidential note cards, etc.) and confirmed arrangements with the White House military office for pick-up and delivery of the finished wreaths. I ordered flowers and greens for the Presidential wreaths, requested an outside storage cooler to keep the wreath materials fresh, and created a work schedule and staffing plan. For many years, staff and outside contractors were hired to work on the holiday weekend to make these wreaths.

In 2014, I saw an opportunity to support the First Lady's Joining Forces Initiative by inviting military families to the White House.

This initiative that supports and honors military families is a key element of her agenda, which she may continue after the President leaves office. My idea was to invite Gold Star family members to help make the official Presidential Memorial Day wreaths, giving them an opportunity to be at the White House on this special weekend that honors the nation's fallen war heroes. Of all the people who would appreciate the chance to work at the White House on this project, this group would find the most meaning. It was an opportunity to link my flower shop volunteer program with an important priority of the First Lady – and to create a very special and meaningful experience for the Gold Star family members.

Working with the First Lady's Joining Forces team, I invited 15 people from national survivor groups to join me in the White House flower shop for the wreath-making project. Many of the family members were planning to be in Washington, D.C. anyway for the Memorial Day weekend. Two of my favorite White House colleagues and friends volunteered to assist me that day – Captain Rosie, a PhD psychologist in the U.S. Army and Master Sergeant Gus, a combat veteran and White House medic. As military personnel and experienced flower shop volunteers, they related well to the Gold Star families.

The Gold Star volunteers arrived at the White House at 9 a.m. on the Saturday before Memorial Day. I planned a full day of activities in the flower shop. We all met in the Visitors' Lobby near the East Entrance. The volunteers introduced themselves and spoke briefly about their fallen loved ones. It was a moving experience that foreshadowed an intense, emotional day. I went over our agenda for the day: in the morning, volunteers helped make the official wreaths that the President places at cemeteries in Washington, D.C. and in the afternoon, each volunteer made a personal wreath to take home in honor of his or her lost loved one. Without a budget for the Gold Star family portion of this event, I purchased the materials for the volunteers' personal memorial wreaths, and their lunch and refreshments. My goal was to ensure that each and every Gold Star family member was honored and appreciated in the way they deserved. I felt strongly that this is what the President and First Lady would expect.

Rosie and Gus helped me set up tables in the small tent adjoining the flower shop where we created work stations for the volunteers. We organized them into 7 teams of 2 people (+1) to make the 7 large official wreaths. The volunteers quickly learned the mechanics of wreath-making – and they were perfectionists – layering in greens, picking flowers, making ribbon bows. They felt so honored to be at the White House, they knew they were representing all Gold Star families, and they wanted their work to shine. At one point, each family member silently placed a symbolic flower on the largest wreath, the one that the President personally places at the Tomb of the Unknown Soldier. In hushed tones, I heard them say that it was important that every Gold Star family member touch the wreath that the President's own hands would touch. Their ritual was poignant and heart-felt. After we completed the official wreaths and shared a brief lunch, the volunteers returned to the work stations to create their personal wreaths. This time, they departed from the rigid military design formula, taking a little more creative license to make wreaths that fully represented their individual loved ones.

The day was filled with tears and laughter, with emotions running the full gamut from raw grief to stoic pride and transcendent grace. It was a remarkable experience and I felt honored to be with them. Many of the volunteers delighted in telling stories and sharing fond memories of their deceased family members, keeping their memories alive through humorous anecdotes and tales of their bravery and achievements. But the pride and laughter invariably gave way to tears of sorrow and loss, especially for the parents who had lost a son or daughter through war. Their sorrow was deep and never-ending. I was especially touched by the couple who moved across the country to Washington, D.C. to be near their son's grave at Arlington Cemetery. Their son was only 19 years old when he died, they said, too young to have many accomplishments under his belt and to have made much of an impact in life or on the battlefield. Their biggest fear was that he would be forgotten. They desperately wanted to ensure that his memory stayed alive and that his life would be honored. Being present at the White House that day was important to them; they said it was an opportunity to honor their son in a way that was both personally meaningful and significant, befitting how he died – an American hero in service to our country.

This type of volunteer collaboration between East Wing staff and the White House flower shop to support a White House policy initiative was unprecedented. Although there was some interaction between the White House culinary team and food and health policy staff, flowers mostly played a silent role at the White

House, serving as a decorative backdrop in the world of official and political diplomacy. Flowers had not been viewed as a tool for supporting a policy goal. Here, they were at the intersection of linking floral symbolism and White House policy on one of America's most solemn days – at our nation's most famous and powerful address.

In this case, not only were the floral elements – the Presidential memorial wreaths – important (symbolizing eternity and national pride) but the way we put them together (with Gold Star family members) was significant, too. They represented the faces of the fallen heroes we honored that day. By linking flowers at the White House for a Presidential holiday ritual with the constituents who experienced the day in the most profoundly personal way, we created symmetry and symbolism – and a powerful moment of floral diplomacy.

And, yes, there is a very personal note to this story. I am also a Gold Star family member, having lost my father when I was only six years old; my youngest sister was only two. My father, CWO Robert Moffett Dowling, was a decorated army pilot who died in combat during the Vietnam War in 1966. When I was growing up, there were no special support programs or counseling for military families, no public recognition or ceremonies for honoring fallen heroes. That day at the White House, I didn't intend to reveal the details about my personal story; I wanted the focus to be on the visiting Gold Star family members. Yet standing there in the White House with this group, it seemed appropriate to tell a volunteer about my father and my family history. Before I knew it, all of the Gold Star volunteers had gathered around me, conveying their understanding of our shared experience living with the legacy of war. The leader of the group pulled a Gold Star pin from her pocket and attached it to my lapel in an impromptu ceremony. "You're one of us," she said, while everyone murmured condolences for my family's loss and took turns to embrace me one by one. It was a lovely, spontaneous gesture of compassion and kindness that I'll never forget.

By midafternoon, the volunteers had completed the special wreaths that honored their loved ones. Rosie, Gus and I walked them to the security gates and exchanged hugs. They were so appreciative and grateful for the experience; each and every person epitomized such profound grace, dignity and strength of human spirit in the face of their personal losses. Of all the projects I was privileged to work on during my White House tenure, this Memorial Day event with Gold Star families stands out as the most rewarding. We created an unforgettable experience for Gold Star family members on the eve of the most important American holiday honoring fallen heroes. We linked the First Lady's policy priority with the White House flower program. We used a new work model that brought the volunteers who would most appreciate the work into the flower shop – creating the ultimate experience of floral diplomacy. And it was an opportunity to honor the memory of my own father, who gave his life in service to our country and who would have been extremely proud of what transpired at the White House that Memorial Day.

ENVIRONMENTAL APPROACH

Over the years, I've learned the importance of appreciating nature and understanding our role in protecting its beauty and sustainability. The simple guidelines of reducing consumption, recycling and re-purposing everyday items confirm that environmentalism relies upon the smart personal choices we make each day. This is especially true in the White House flower shop because flowers – as elements of nature – make an inherent statement about the environment that is magnified on the White House stage. At the White House, floral choices are scrutinized for meaning and impact, raising questions: Where are the flowers from (imported or locally grown)? How were they transported (with a high or low carbon foot-print)? How are they grown (organically or with pesticides)? What happens to them after their use (re-cycled or composted)? Hence, a paramount goal of the flower shop was to make beautiful bouquets and decorations but in an environmentally-friendly manner. Many of the flowers we used were sustainably harvested and either locally grown on nearby farms or American-grown and were placed in organic vases we made from recycled leaves and greens.

We also endeavored to recycle and re-purpose existing designs and use easily available natural materials that are either inexpensive or free. Using natural materials from the garden, other simple elements and items from the White House collection, we created interesting décor that could be replicated simply and easily at very low cost by all Americans at home. The White House offsite warehouse contained ornaments and decorations dating back decades from which we could discover beautiful materials to use, including vintage collections from previous administrations, a treasure trove of American artistry and patriotic history. By refurbishing and integrating these wonderful elements from the White House "attic" – Betty Ford's satin ornaments, Nancy Reagan's red cardinal birds, Laura Bush's gold gilded leaves and beaded faux fruit, etc., we could take classic elements and turn them into fresh, contemporary designs – just like most Americans do every year with their own interior and holiday decor. It was an important message and a good example to set every day. An added plus for our philosophy of re-using and recycling existing decor was that it was much more cost-effective than purchasing an entire set of new decorations ever year.

In addition to recycling and repurposing existing designs for the holiday seasons, floral designs for state dinners and other official events were occasions where the flowers could make environmental statements. For instance, the domestic floral choices for the France state dinner made a statement of support of the American Cut Flower Industry, highlighting the advantages and beauty of locally-grown and sustainably harvested flowers. A luncheon in the East Room in honor of the winners of the Smithsonian's prestigious Cooper Hewitt Design Awards featured seasonal flowers from local farms. Here, the choice of flowers sourced from nearby farms made a strong statement of support not only for American flower farmers but for an environmentally-friendly approach to growing, cutting, and transporting flowers. On an everyday basis, our use of simple natural materials to craft intricate patterns and motifs for vases to display flower arrangements signaled an underlying environmental theme and approach to design.

THE GREEN ROOM.

During the holiday season, we featured environmentally-friendly decorations in the Green Room to highlight a "green" approach to White House flowers and décor. Many of the bouquets and other decorative items were repurposed and recycled. In 2010, we created large gilded trees made from newspaper cones that were painted gold and attached to underlying structures. These were complemented by large hand-made wreaths for the windows made out of strips of looped newspapers which were also painted and glittered with gold, and displayed using natural cedar roping. More recycled paper elements – trees made out of folded magazine pages, floral containers made from newspaper – carried out the message of recycling. The projects required so much newspaper – hundreds of pounds – I asked colleagues to bring in their recycled newspapers to help. It was a fun and collaborative effort involving dozens of White House staff and volunteers. The annual Home and Garden Television (HGTV) special on the White House holidays featured an interview with the volunteer who worked on the project, who gave a step-by-step tutorial on how to duplicate the designs at home. This added an important educational element to the mix. The trees turned out beautifully and were featured on several design blogs. It was always our goal to create décor that inspired people. A bonus was the ability to highlight the important environmental theme of recycling and creative re-use.

The following year, we came up with an even more ambitious environmentally-themed concept for Green Room holiday décor. My concept was architecturally inspired pyramids made of recycled soft-drink cans enhanced with boxwood trim. Given their position in the Green Room overlooking the South Lawn, I wanted to create a classic form that referenced historic garden ornamentation. We used recycled aluminum cans to create the two large pyramid-shaped trees, matching topiaries and silver-toned wreaths. I embarked on a comprehensive proposal and planning process, creating sketches and prototype designs and receiving necessary budgetary approvals to launch the environmentally-friendly recycling theme.

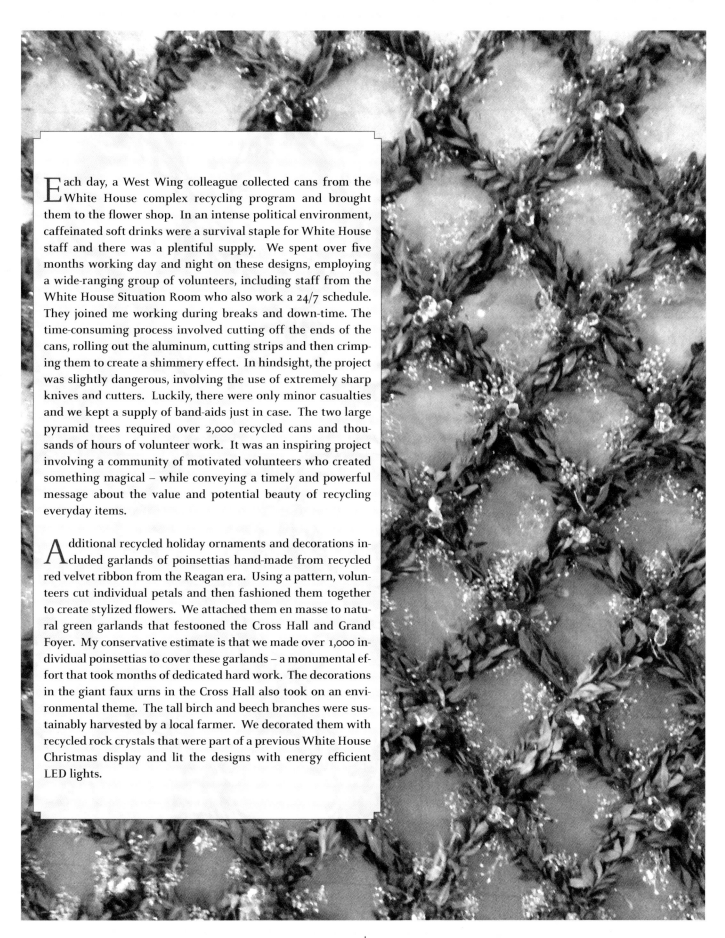

Each day, a West Wing colleague collected cans from the White House complex recycling program and brought them to the flower shop. In an intense political environment, caffeinated soft drinks were a survival staple for White House staff and there was a plentiful supply. We spent over five months working day and night on these designs, employing a wide-ranging group of volunteers, including staff from the White House Situation Room who also work a 24/7 schedule. They joined me working during breaks and down-time. The time-consuming process involved cutting off the ends of the cans, rolling out the aluminum, cutting strips and then crimping them to create a shimmery effect. In hindsight, the project was slightly dangerous, involving the use of extremely sharp knives and cutters. Luckily, there were only minor casualties and we kept a supply of band-aids just in case. The two large pyramid trees required over 2,000 recycled cans and thousands of hours of volunteer work. It was an inspiring project involving a community of motivated volunteers who created something magical – while conveying a timely and powerful message about the value and potential beauty of recycling everyday items.

Additional recycled holiday ornaments and decorations included garlands of poinsettias hand-made from recycled red velvet ribbon from the Reagan era. Using a pattern, volunteers cut individual petals and then fashioned them together to create stylized flowers. We attached them en masse to natural green garlands that festooned the Cross Hall and Grand Foyer. My conservative estimate is that we made over 1,000 individual poinsettias to cover these garlands – a monumental effort that took months of dedicated hard work. The decorations in the giant faux urns in the Cross Hall also took on an environmental theme. The tall birch and beech branches were sustainably harvested by a local farmer. We decorated them with recycled rock crystals that were part of a previous White House Christmas display and lit the designs with energy efficient LED lights.

One of my all-time favorite projects was the gilded oak leaf door surrounds we made for the East Entrance. I was inspired by the Italianate windows on a circa 1820 historic house in my Alexandria, Virginia neighborhood. Every day on my way to work I would pass by this house and admire the design and craftsmanship, especially the exquisite architectural detail. The shape of the window surround was stunning and elegant – the perfect inspiration for White House holiday decorations. My starting point was to photograph the window and transfer it to a plywood form. I asked volunteers to bring in fallen oak leaves from their gardens and neighborhoods to use to make the rosettes. Each rosette took 25 leaves that were rolled and crafted to look like a stylized rose. These were then gilded and dipped in gold glitter. We made approximately 2,000 rosettes that were applied to the Italianate forms, which were anchored by a plinth made of gilded pinecone scales. It was a wonderful (and time-consuming) project. What made the project so satisfying for me was that the impressive scale of the design was easily accessible: anyone could gather leaves from their yard and pinecones from the woods to duplicate the look.

Finally, as a complement to the environmental motifs, we filled the green room with seasonal flowers and natural decorations, including bouquets in hand-made magnolia leaf and pine cone containers, berry-covered vases and other garden-inspired elements. Through the flower program, an intrinsic theme in the White House throughout the Obama presidency (and especially in the Green Room) was to enhance the connection and appreciation of nature's beauty.

INNOVATION

During my years of White House service, technological innovations transformed the way we worked and communicated with each other – from e-mail and Blackberries to digital and graphics technology – the advent of new technology at the White House impacted everything from how I ordered flowers to how I presented design schemes to the First Lady. It was a time of transformational change. At the same time, it was clear that the importance of technology and innovation was a priority of the President. Under President Obama, the Office of Science and Technology Policy (OSTP) was elevated to a key advisory role. Whatever is important to the President is – by extension – important to the staff. With this philosophy as a guiding principle and knowing that the First Lady expected flowers to support White House programs, I devoted quite a bit of thought to the question of how to merge technology and design. Through the strategic use of symbolic flowers and décor, we were already supporting many White House initiatives and missions, including Let's Move and Joining Forces while promoting an overarching environmental awareness and conservation ethic. My role evolved gradually over the years, culminating in an exciting strategic partnership with the technology and innovation teams in 2014 – the creation of robotic replicas of the First Family's dogs.

BO AND SUNNY INSPIRATION.

Little did Sunny and Bo know while romping happily around the White House grounds or meandering through the Executive Mansion that their faux versions would morph into amazing characters made in the flower shop first as holiday "ornaments" and then to eventually promote technology and education. Each year, I organized a group of volunteers to make stylized versions of them on special chicken-wire frames made by a craftsman in California based on measurements of the actual dogs taken by an architect who volunteered in the flower shop. Initially, there was only Bo, and the first versions (pipe cleaner Bo, pom-pom Bo and trash bag Bo) were immobile and presented as art pieces for young visitors to enjoy.

The simple materials we used to put them together along with the army of volunteers who made them fostered a compelling narrative of creative achievement about what is possible when people work together towards a common goal. Each volunteer played an important role in the ultimate success of these projects whether they worked for weeks or months or just for a few hours on a weekend afternoon. They all had a stake in the outcome and felt proud to be part of something that was bigger than their individual roles. Eventually Sunny appeared on the scene. She was dutifully measured and reproduced in black ribbon in various playful poses; faux versions of both dogs appeared in the Booksellers area of the White House and on the South Lawn dressed up for Halloween. Given the popularity and visibility of these dog topiaries, it was obvious that the project would be a permanent fixture during upcoming holiday seasons. It also became apparent that there was potential to amplify the project's reach and impact by linking the design to a larger strategic message.

A CREATIVE CHALLENGE.

Each year, we had to outdo ourselves in creativity and originality as we contemplated the annual holiday replicas of First Dogs Sunny and Bo. For the first few years, the dogs stood as statues covered in ribbon and other black and white materials – including pipe cleaners, licorice, buttons and marshmallows. In 2013, we upped the ante and proposed adding movement to the design in the form of wagging tails for Bo and Sunny. This would be a new innovation. Working with the in-house carpenters and electricians, we came up with a plan to motorize the dogs' tails before we added the ruched ribbon covering. The electricians installed a motor that they removed from a lawn reindeer – the kind that are sold inexpensively at dime stores. They rigged the motor with a coat hanger and rubber band that the carpenters attached to the frame with a wooden block. It was definitely a low-tech solution. Their first iteration had the dogs moving their tails very slowly, in slow motion, as if they were sedated. The electricians tweaked the motor, speeding it up so that the wag resembled something more like a real-life dog. My volunteers and I then covered the dogs with looped satin ribbon, leaving a space on the hind end near the tail for the electricians to access the motor and attach an electrical cord.

The dogs were placed on their platform in the Booksellers area of the White House – a ground floor room that connects the East Colonnade with the main Executive Residence. They sat there throughout the holiday season, much to the delight of visitors who took photographs and video of the animatronic dogs. Everything was going well until one morning late into the season. As I made my morning walk through to check on the decorations, I noticed that Bo's tail was twitching instead of wagging as if it was caught on something. Upon closer inspection, I noticed that smoke was coming out of Bo's tail with small sparks flying everywhere. The ribbon was caught in the motor and about to ignite. I pulled the plug just in time before disaster could strike – and Bo and Sunny became motionless for the rest of the season.

TECHNOLOGY, EDUCATION AND DESIGN.

The following year, in 2014, we took faux Bo and Sunny to the next level. Using robotics technology, we created robotic, artistic representations of the Obamas' pet dogs, whom we referred to as "Bo-bots". They were made of miles of "Bo-fur" attached to chicken wire frames that featured moving heads and motion sensor eyes. They became projects of great scale and ambition. Bo-bots were the culmination of my years-long effort to bring in strategic partners and international guest designers for training and events, as well as to foster creative collaborations with artists from all disciplines. Our collaborations included partnerships with the American Institute of Floral Designers, Presidential Innovation Fellows, and the Office of Science and Technology Policy teams. By having florists, artisans, innovators and scientists work together, we created designs that expanded visitors' everyday holiday experiences at the White House through the application of cutting-edge technology. In the course of just a few years, faux Bo and Sunny advanced from being stationary statues, to dogs whose tails wagged (and sometimes smoked), and finally to dogs whose heads tracked the movements of visitors, especially children, who were their biggest and most curious fans. Applied technology made faux Bo and Sunny lifelike and interesting, and created new opportunities for linking design with Science, Technology, Engineering and Math (STEM) education, a priority of the Obama Administration. That October and November the flower shop became a multi-disciplinary laboratory of creativity and intellectual excitement; a community of volunteers who were each motivated to contribute their small part to the overall effort. This was collaborative floral diplomacy at its finest.

"BO-BOTS," ETC.

The behind-the-scenes process for creating the Bo-bots was fascinating. I was inspired by a "Let's Move" video that showed the First Family dogs, Bo and Sunny, sitting together in the Lower Cross Hall as the President and Vice President ran by, the dogs' heads moving in unison back and forth. I wanted to duplicate that movement in the ribbon-covered replica dogs, making their heads swivel on the frame, using computer technology. The question was how. The in-house carpenters and electricians opted out of the equation, noting that robotics were "above their pay grade." Then I learned about a team of White House technology experts, West Wing colleagues who focus on science and innovation, technology and education as part of their mission to advise the President on these issues. I reached out to them to brainstorm ideas about integrating new technologies into the 2014 holiday décor scheme.

We started talking about ideas in July and August, well before the holidays and when most people were thinking about beach vacations rather than holiday decor. In a special "innovation room" located in the White House complex that featured groupings of tables and chairs and high-tech computer equipment surrounded by a low-tech "white board" for writing down ideas, we came up with some exciting options for a collaboration that would integrate new technologies with our holiday designs. The first idea: The team suggested hosting a 3D printing ornament contest that would allow people from across the country to compete for the honor of displaying their winning ornament on the White House holiday trees. 3D printing technology was becoming more accessible and mainstream with a wide range of industrial and design applications. It would be fun and innovative to bring this technology to White House design. Five winning designs would be chosen to be featured during the holiday period which would then be donated to the Smithsonian to go on permanent display.

Another idea involved introducing cutting edge interactive digital technology into White House holiday décor. This technology, which uses 3D modeling and rendering tools, captures the outlines and movements of visitors, projecting them on the wall as a flurry of snowflakes in an enchanting snow-covered forest scene. White House visitors would actually become part of the holiday décor. Technically, it requires setting up cameras with motion sensors along with computers and digital projectors to capture images and translate them into an interactive digital scene. The more visitors move, the more snowflakes are displayed.

We partnered with a Portland, Oregon-based firm that received a grant from the National Endowment for the Arts to create this innovative holiday installation.

We discussed building the robotic dogs which was the project everyone was most excited about. Given the scope of work, we needed to start immediately. The division of labor fell along design and technical lines: I would handle the design side, procure the chicken wire frames, order the ribbon for the fur, and gather teams of volunteers to begin work on the arduous task of creating miles of looped ribbon "Bo-fur." Meanwhile, the technical teams would develop and install the robotic parts.

There were two technical teams: the Office of Science and Technology Policy (OSTP) staff created Bo's robotic head. The Presidential Innovation Fellows (PIFs) took on Sunny. Both teams volunteered their time and donated robotic components since there was no holiday budget for this initiative. So the Bo-bot and Sunny-bot volunteers purchased inexpensive parts via mail order and manufactured additional parts themselves. I was surprised to learn that anyone could purchase Arduino robot motors for about $25 online at Amazon. That in itself was inspiring. Both teams retro-fitted the chicken wire frames with these small servomotors that powered the swivel platforms.

I noticed that both teams used rubber bands to attach the motor to the frame, causing me to flashback to "Smoking-tail Bo" from the previous year. They assured me that there would be no smoking heads or tails with their designs. From the beginning, there was a spirit of camaraderie (and friendly competition) between the teams. The high-spirited Bo team was comprised of a PhD Information Scientist, a software genius with experience in the gaming world, and a talented graduate intern. Team Bo integrated some custom-designed 3D-printed pieces in their design, a great nod to the "maker" movement – the DIY trend that uses creative skills to make or design products. Their initial design focused on creating a swivel platform that turned 360 degrees around and around – Bo's head looked more like "The Exorcist" than the cute and friendly dog I envisioned in the "Let's Move" video. We all laughed at Bo's fully revolving head. They kept tweaking the arc of the swivel to look natural (and less scary) and stabilized the platform holding the motor in order to reduce torque (and thus wear and tear on the motor). The team programmed software to control the speed, angle and sequence of Bo's head rotation. The "Bo-bot" was nearly complete.

Meanwhile, the Sunny team was off and running. Like their OSTP colleagues, the PIFs also brought impressive skills to the table. They were computer entrepreneurs from Silicon Valley with extensive programming experience. In addition to the robotic heads, the Sunny team introduced the idea of motion sensors – small chips connected to Sunny's eyes that would track guests as they walked by the display, causing the dog's head to move as if following the visitors. They also had the idea of programming a sequence of varying head movements – a routine that essentially involved Sunny shaking her head at different speeds and intervals. They even floated an idea for making the Sunny-bot interactive on social media, including Facebook and Twitter.

Both teams worked with me in the flower shop, joining me in the evening after they got off work. While the technical team worked on the robotic dogs, the "Bo-fur" team created garland. For months, volunteers created miles of looped black and white satin ribbon garlands that would be applied to the chicken wire frames. For this project, we created an all hands on deck situation, inviting anyone who had some free time to join in on the project. As we edged closer to our deadlines, larger groups of volunteers assisted with the project. In fact, many of the PIFs – when they heard about the exciting robotic dog holiday project from their colleagues – were eager to join the team. It was amazing to watch the progress unfold. Team Sunny experimented with the speed and trajectory of the swivel, creating several different movement sequences. They researched actual dog movements to program a coordinated routine. When I looked over at them, they were moving their heads – tilted on the same angle as the replica – swiveling back and forth in unison – imitating the motion they wanted to reproduce. It was hilarious. For several weeks, both teams worked late into the night to fine tune and perfect the technical details, make adjustments, and replace motors as needed. Once the robotic components were in place, it was time for the "Bo-fur" team to swing into action and apply the miles of ribbon garland to the frames. It was great to have some of the best and the brightest technical minds in America in the flower shop creating these designs at the juncture of technology, design, and White House tradition. They not only brought technical knowledge and skill to this project but demonstrated an approach to the work that was entrepreneurial, creative and inspirational.

When guests entered the area with the interactive digital snow-scape and "Bo-bot" displays, they saw something new, unexpected and magical. As they walked by a large screen hanging on the East wall of the Booksellers area, they could interact with a beautiful snowy landscape. When they walked in front of the projector, the outline of their body was projected onto the screen as a stylized snowy figure. Visitors were mesmerized by the technology that allowed them to move their arms and legs, and jump in the air while the movement was projected on the screen. Meanwhile, directly across the room, the Bo-bots were on display and moving their heads back and forth much to the delight of onlookers, especially children. It was truly a display of high-tech magic at the White House that captured the spirit of the season. It also created another template for linking White House design with applied technology and administration priorities. While the technology we used for the "Bo-bots" was not complex, the nexus with custom design and artistic details allowed us to create something very special. Public interest generated by the designs was phenomenal. The White House teams used social media technology to interact with groups of school children, giving them a how-to tutorial on how to make robotic dogs. The next iteration of these projects could include educational and interactive components (e.g., open source coding) to make White House designs accessible to all. In the end, this project was an example of how floral diplomacy embraced technology and education and came out. . . . swiveling.

BEHIND THE SCENES

EVERYDAY FLOWERS

Walking through the majestic state floors and period rooms of the White House year after year was a privilege that never got old or ceased to amaze me. No matter where I went in the course of my work, I was reminded of those who lived and worked there and walked the hallowed halls before me. What always surprised me was how intimate and livable the space is – the perfectly-proportioned human scale of the White House. French diplomat and political thinker Alexis de Tocqueville famously said that "the President occupies a palace that in Paris would be called a fine private residence." How befitting of a democratic nation with egalitarian ideals. Even though the ceilings are high (almost 19 ft.) and the furnishings are priceless, there is a sense of accessibility and an innate welcoming quality not found in the homes or castles of other heads of state. The flowers served to enhance this feeling. I found endless inspiration in White House architect James Hoban's classical design: friezes, medallions, patterns, columns and motifs – that I often incorporated into my floral bouquets, container designs and holiday decorations. Perhaps my favorite room in the White House for displaying flowers was the Blue Room. With its distinctive oval-shape, American and French

furnishings, and striking cobalt-blue color, it exudes a feeling of timeless splendor. Here, the large focal point bouquet in the center of the room sets the tone of understated, accessible elegance that echoes throughout the White House.

My main job was to create everyday flowers for the White House complex, including the main Executive Mansion and the East and West Wing Offices. Traditionally, bouquets are placed throughout the route that visitors take on a White House tour – from the desk at the East Entrance past the ground floor rooms, the Library and the Vermeil rooms, to the State Floor, where flowers were featured in the Green Room, Blue Room, Red Room and State Dining Room. The flowers add beauty, bring the garden indoors and complement the historic architecture while softening the formality of the period rooms. On the public tour route, the flowers take on an ambassadorial role, drawing people in and creating common ground. The fancy antique furnishings are perhaps too far removed from most people's lives. But the flowers are readily approachable, easing visitors into the rarefied White House world and making them feel welcome.

FLOWERS ON THE STATE FLOORS.

The flowers on the state floors – the ground floor and main floor of the White House – are an opportunity to involve visitors and make them feel special – in the spirit that Mrs. Obama initially envisioned and that Jacqueline Kennedy spear-headed almost 60 years ago. My approach to decorating these rooms was simple. I employed a changing array of flowers and colors to highlight the season and to set a warm, welcoming tone. My goal was to design garden-style bouquets that showcased the features of each room – the architecture, the colors and furnishings, and the spirit (e.g., whether it was formal or casual, majestic or intimate). Over the years, I saw which colors worked best in the rooms – blue, purple and fuchsia in the Blue Room, shades of plum and red in the Red Room, green and white in the Green Room, soft pinks and creams in the State Dining Room. But I never stopped with just one formula or design for these rooms. A surprising feature of the White House is that despite the strong shades of vivid colors in the rooms, many color combinations (including some unusual ones) were perfectly at home. Each week, we created new designs and different combinations of flowers to give energy and life to the rooms. Although it would have been easier to make one design and repeat it with a standing order of flowers each week, the constantly changing designs (and hand-made organic containers) were a hallmark of my approach. It lent an air of excitement to the flower program, a feeling of possibility and a sense of anticipation about what would be next.

On the public tour route, the flowers became a topic of discussion. Secret Service agents serve as de facto tour guides, answering questions about the White House furnishings and décor – and often, the flowers. One time an agent told me about an incident where two women leaned over the ropes to admire a Blue Room arrangement. "Be careful," the agent warned, "there's a camera and listening device inside." "What? You're kidding!" they responded, jumping away from the flowers. Of course he was joking. Or was he? The agents are well-versed on the history of flowers at the White House and often tell fascinating stories like the one they recount about Franklin Pierce who served as President from 1853 – 1857. As the story goes, President Pierce, in an effort to help his wife overcome overwhelming and debilitating grief after the death of their young son, started placing flowers in the state floor rooms in an effort to lure her out of seclusion. His use of flowers as a tool to fight depression and gloom with beauty in the wake of their personal tragedy is credited with launching the tradition of exhibiting flowers in the White House public spaces. Years later, Jacqueline Kennedy ushered in the modern era of the White House flower program, establishing the office of the Chief Floral Designer in 1961. Mrs. Kennedy's fashion and style sense is well-known. She is credited with restoring the White House, meticulously collecting and displaying American antiques, making the White House a showcase of American decorative arts. Early on, she realized the power of flowers to create a first impression: while many of the renovations and restorations would take time, she knew that bouquets in the rooms would make a strong aesthetic statement. They would be the best and quickest way to showcase a new American style. The former First Lady was inspired by the French aesthetic in floral design featuring free-flowing lines of seasonal flowers and vines emanating from classical French bouquets, displayed in Chinese export porcelain bowls and gilded vermeil urns. Mrs. Kennedy believed that the natural French garden style was timeless, beautiful and appropriate for the White House. I have always been inspired by her visionary approach. Through flowers and décor, my goal was to honor cherished traditions of the White House while highlighting the best of American spirit and support the current First Lady's vision to make the White House the "People's House."

THE PRIVATE WHITE HOUSE.

In addition to the flowers for the public spaces, I managed flowers for the private quarters of the First Family. The President said that the flowers are his favorite thing about living in the White House, so I always viewed this aspect of the portfolio as the site of our most important work. In this historic setting where Presidents and their families have lived for over 200 years, the flowers help create a serene ambiance, a personal oasis and a place they can call home. Here, the President and First Lady can relax away from the glare of the public eye and media scrutiny. Early on in the Obama Administration, we mapped out a template that focused on designing flowers in key areas: the elevator vestibule, the west sitting hall, the dining room, center hall, office and bedrooms. In general, the design strategy repeated the garden-style approach that I used on the state floors below. But since the residence incorporates contemporary furniture and modern art, the flowers also featured contemporary twists such as monochromatic colors, art glass vases, and simple tall branches. Bouquets were changed every week according to the season, featuring flowers from local farms, including zinnias, dahlias, sunflowers, hydrangea and garden roses.

As the home of the First Family, the private residence was the site of many special occasions over the years. Both the President and First Lady appreciated the flowers and often called on me to create flowers to celebrate special holidays and family milestones: birthdays, Valentine's Day, Mother's Day, Thanksgiving and other events. In a speech at the White House in February 2012, the President said "For all the gentlemen out there, today is Valentine's Day. Do not forget. I speak from experience here; it is important that you remember this and go big. This is my advice." Heeding his own holiday advice, the President requested special Valentine's bouquets that we delivered to his wife, daughters and mother-in-law that day. During another interview about Valentine's Day, a reporter asked the First Lady if the President used his credit card to order flowers like out of a scene from the movie "The American President." She laughed and said, "no, that doesn't happen. He just calls downstairs for flowers – they're really good there."

Both the President and First Lady celebrated their 50th birthdays at the White House. The festivities for the President's 50th birthday, in early August 2011, began with a barbecue dinner in the Rose Garden on a sweltering and muggy day. A summery spread of chicken, ribs, hamburgers, hot dogs, pasta salad and four kinds of pies was laid out on long buffet tables for the guests. To carry out the summer theme, I created casual bouquets of sunflowers, chamomile and mimosa in terra cotta pots. What happened next is somewhat in dispute. Allegedly, the White House honey bees, agitated from an event in the garden that day, were not properly "locked up" in advance of the party. Free to roam the White House grounds, they crashed the party, swarming the sunflowers along with the unsuspecting guests. One staff member, known for his dramatic flair and excitable embellishments, described a scene of chaos with angry bees, fueled by the sunflowers' nectar, charging and chasing guests back and forth across the Rose Garden. Another staffer, with a more relaxed demeanor, professed to not see bees or anything unusual going on at all. Nevertheless, the butlers, erring on the safe side, pulled the sunflowers from the tables and brought them indoors. After dinner, the party moved to the East Room for a late night of revelry and dancing with Stevie Wonder serenading the guests. It was an un-bee-lieveable event.

The First Lady's 50th birthday in January 2014 was fortunately a calmer, but no less festive affair. The invitation signaled it would be an evening of dancing and included a polite instruction to eat before they arrived. However, the buffet menu of mini-crab cakes, fried oysters, roast beef sliders and champagne was on tap for hungry revelers. There were over 500 guests in attendance, many of whom were celebrities including Sir Paul McCartney, Gladys Knight, and Michael Jordan as well as luminaries from the political world: Bill and Hillary Clinton, House Speaker Nancy Pelosi, and Vice President Joe Biden. The dance party was held in the East Room. Beyonce performed a medley of her hits including "All the Single Ladies" while John Legend was given the honor of serenading the First Lady with a jazzy performance of "Happy Birthday." To complement the glittery affair, we created modern, graphic white and green floral displays in chic black vases. The First Lady's birthday also had a bee theme. With a show-stopping performance, the Queen Bee – Beyonce – ensured that it was an unforgettable evening.

PRIVATE RESIDENCE OFFICIAL EVENTS.

The private residence is also the venue for important official meetings, receptions and events. When a foreign dignitary visits the White House, it is customary for the First Lady to host the spouse in the Yellow Oval Room for a luncheon or tea. These events call for additional flower arrangements, including a presentation bouquet that the First Lady gives to her guest at the conclusion of the tea.

TEA WITH THE FIRST LADY

Russia

Mrs. Obama welcomed Mrs. Svetlana Medvedeva, First Lady of Russia, to a special luncheon in the Yellow Oval Room in June, 2010. When First Ladies visit the private residence, there is a heightened sense of importance. The private residence is set with special flowers created in honor of the guest, including a focal point piece in the Center Hall. Often times these flowers are designed to take on symbolic significance. For this event, I incorporated sunflowers. In the 18th century, Russian Czar Peter the Great became enthralled with the sunflowers he saw in the Netherlands. He brought back seeds that Russian farmers began planting to grow over 2 million acres of sunflowers. By 1880, Russian immigrants brought the large "mammoth Russian sunflower" with them to the U.S. where it was grown and propagated and advertised in American seed catalogues. The story of the Russian sunflower is an example of floral and cultural exchange that I used to create special bouquets in honor of the Russian First Lady. To create the symbolic display, I started with an organic container: leaves from the White House grounds that were rolled into cylinders and glued onto a base and then gilded with gold paint. The main bouquet was an array of sunflowers mixed with foliage and trailing passion flower vines. I accented this centerpiece with 4 lemon topiaries presented in the collection of gilded vermeil urns. The lemons were a colorful complement to the sunflowers and created a cheery display of yellow floral diplomacy on a warm spring day.

Israel

The Prime Minister of Israel, Benjamin Netanyahu, has visited the White House several times in recent years, often accompanied by his wife Mrs. Sara Netanyahu. During a visit in July 2010, Mrs. Obama invited Mrs. Netanyahu to join her for tea in the Yellow Oval Room. I proposed a rainbow theme for the Center Hall décor. The rainbow is a universal symbol of peace and harmony and I felt it was an appropriate message for a close friend and ally. We carried out the rainbow theme creating chevron ribbon vases, made of folded bands of satin ribbon. I filled these vases with flowers that were arranged in bands of color to resemble the colors of the rainbow. The technique for making a rainbow-patterned bouquet is different from a typical garden style approach. Instead of alternating layers of mixed flowers and foliage, the flowers are stacked in definitive stripes of color. To complement the colorful display, we placed brightly hued bouquets in the Yellow Oval Room where the First Ladies would sit down for tea. The theme of floral harmony and international diplomacy continued over a cup of tea.

Greece

Each year, the President and First Lady host a reception in honor of Greek Independence Day, featuring a Greek menu, Greek-themed décor (blue and white flowers and linens in honor of the colors of the Greek flag). In March 2010, Mrs. Obama hosted a tea in honor of Mrs. Ada Papandreou in the Yellow Oval Room prior to the event. The Yellow Oval Room décor featured bold multi-colored bouquets to evoke the flowers that bloom on the Greek Islands, immortalized in stories of Greek Mythology. In the Center Hall, I created a yellow-themed display of roses, orchids, olive branches and rosemary, along with lemon topiaries, another allusion to friendship and the landscape of Greece.

Denmark

The day after the Germany state dinner, on June 8, 2011, the Queen of Denmark (Marguerite) visited the White House for a private tea with the First Lady. It was the second visit of a European dignitary in two days and once again flowers played a role in the event. Queen Marguerite is called "Daisy" in her home country – and her favorite flower is also the daisy. So a little daisy bouquet was the obvious choice for the presentation bouquet. Since I knew that I would be at my flower class in Germany on the day of the event, I prepared all of the flowers ahead of time: flowers for the Center Hall, Yellow Oval Room and a presentation bouquet of simple white daisies, wrapped in greens and trailing vines and tied with a coordinating satin ribbon. Everything was designed and ready for placement on the morning of the tea, with the daisy bouquet presented on a silver platter. It was an example of personalized floral diplomacy.

PRESIDENT BUSH PORTRAIT UNVEILING.

In May 2012, two former U.S. Presidents, George W. Bush and George H.W. Bush, along with their families, came to the White House for the unveiling of the official George W. and Laura Bush portraits. It's a special White House tradition; the current president hosts the most recent President and First Lady for a ceremonial unveiling of their portraits in the East Room, followed by a luncheon on the State Floor. Approximately 200 invited guests, including former staffers, friends and colleagues were invited to attend the unveiling. George W. Bush has kept a relatively low profile since leaving office, taking up painting and enjoying his time at the family ranch in Crawford, Texas. He was in a relaxed and jovial mood that day. In his remarks, President Bush said that the addition of his portrait brings "interesting symmetry" to the White House collection: there will now be two "George W.s."

He went on to recount the story of Dolly Madison's heroic efforts to save the famous Gilbert Stuart portrait of George Washington as the British burned the White House in 1814. Turning to Mrs. Obama, he said slyly, "Michelle, if anything happens, there's your man," gesturing to his newly revealed portrait. The room full of friends and family members – as well as the President and First Lady – burst into raucous laughter.

After the official ceremony, the two former President Bushes and their immediate families strolled through the Cross Hall to the Red Room that was set for the luncheon. To honor the Bush family, I proposed using one of the most beautiful sets of Presidential china – the hand-painted "Magnolia" china commissioned by First Lady Laura Bush near the end of the Bush Administration. The china pattern features a whimsical depiction of foliage and insects, rendered in exquisite hand-painted detail by a Hungarian-American artist. Its classic garden style motif in shades of green, pink, lilac, and cream blends beautifully with a wide range of floral designs. The Magnolia china is a relatively small service, only 70 place settings, so it is ideal for intimate White House gatherings. And it was a perfect touch for the Bush family event. I also designed special floral décor to honor the former President and First Lady. During their 8 years in the White House, they both favored bright orange and coral roses for their floral decorations so I incorporated these flowers into all of the table designs. For this special event, the symbolic gathering of two former Presidents with the current President showcased the strength of American democracy – the coming together to honor the institution of the Presidency, no matter political differences or party affiliations. The décor and flowers helped to support that message.

OTHER SPECIAL OCCASIONS.

The White House is always a popular place for momentous occasions, especially engagements. The Blue Room is by far the most popular site for a White House matrimonial proposal. Some visitors and White House staff are even savvy enough to enlist colleagues and Secret Service members in their romantic plots. I remember one time when a senior staff member in the West Wing requested my help with his plan to propose to his girlfriend in the Rose Garden. The plan went as follows: on the appointed day around 6 p.m., he would stop by the flower shop with his girlfriend, pick up a small bouquet (made from flowers he purchased), and then head over to the Rose Garden to pop the question. Two of his colleagues would be stationed at each end of the Colonnade that connects the West Wing with the Palm Room, with the task of stopping unwitting staffers from entering the space until the deed was done. Unfortunately, things went a little awry straight away. When the couple came by the flower shop to pick up the flowers, I made a not-too-convincing explanation that the flower shop hands out flowers to certain special White House visitors. She seemed perplexed at that thought of free flower hand-outs, but happily accepted the bouquet. Then, one of my chatty volunteers (blithely unaware of the life-changing moment at hand), peppered the jittery groom-to-be with a barrage of questions. "What are you two up to?" "What are the flowers for?" I could see that the senior staffer was becoming increasingly agitated – clearly not the right mood for an impending proposal. In a attempt to salvage the plot and maintain the element of surprise – and interject a little floral diplomacy – I changed the conversation and steered them towards the door. Then they were on their way.

What happened next unfolded like a scene out of a television comedy. The groom-to-be and his unsuspecting bride, standing in position in the colonnade overlooking the Rose Garden, were apparently repeatedly interrupted as he tried to carry out his plan for a romantic proposal. His friends were delayed (or forgot) to stand sentry at the entrance, which meant random people continued to wander past them, invading their privacy and killing the romantic mood. In what must have seemed like rush hour in the West Wing, more than a dozen colleagues walked back and forth through the colonnade at that critical moment, giving the couple quizzical looks as they stood there awkwardly. "Hey A., what's goin' on?" one guy asked, casually tossing a football in the air while simultaneously checking his Blackberry. The President's speechwriter walked by with a bourbon in hand, inviting A. to join him for a drink. Just as A. started in with his proposal, the First Lady's Chief of Staff strolled up and attempted to engage the couple in friendly conversation, which A. had to cut short. Meanwhile, A.'s friend assumed his guard position, hiding behind a bush so as not be seen. Just as A. started in with his proposal spiel, another person walked by. Finally, exasperated, the groom just popped the question, his girlfriend accepted, and there was finally a happy ending to the story. The speechwriter, returning to his desk, had alerted colleagues in the West Wing about what he suspected was a marriage proposal, which launched an impromptu receiving line in the lobby. The flowers that had seemed so random and tangential before ("a special giveaway for White House visitors"), now took on relevant significance. It was another instance of carrying out White House floral diplomacy one bouquet at a time.

THE TRUMAN BALCONY.

Another time, Mrs. Obama asked for my help with the planters on the Truman Balcony. In good weather, the First Family often spends time there and the plants create a lovely garden feeling and a sense of privacy. I sketched out a couple of different plans and color schemes featuring bouquet-style plantings for her to review – large focal point flowers and topiaries, including yellow hibiscus standards, with coordinating under plantings and trailing elements such as mandevilla, sweet potato and passionflower. The planters were designed to resemble my bouquets – colorful and lively with different heights, dancing branches and floating butterflies. Mrs. Obama selected a complementary color scheme of purple, lilac and yellow flowers with lime green accents. With the help of groundskeepers who are responsible for plants and flowers on the Truman Balcony, we added some new colors, textures and types of flowers into the typical White House mix, creating a personalized, private oasis in this iconic space that the First Family could enjoy.

FLOWERS IN
THE EAST AND WEST WINGS.

A former White House staffer once said: working in the White House means the longest days and shortest years of your life – a poignant and apt description of the White House experience. For most employees, it's an intense and stressful 24/7 job with few opportunities for relaxation or balance between work and family life. Flowers help to create a calming mood. Except for the Oval Office, where the bouquets are often photographed as the backdrop to official Presidential business, most of the flowers in the East and West Wings are placed out of sight, tucked away in a labyrinth of private offices. They provide a touch of beauty and a private moment of inspiration for the recipients as they perform their jobs in an exceptionally challenging environment. My goal was always to deliver beautiful flowers to my White House colleagues – executed with thoughtfulness, attention to detail, and stylistic flair, changing every week with no two ever alike, and reflecting each season throughout the year.

Nowhere was the impact of the bouquets more evident than in the West Wing lobby where ROTUS (the receptionist of the United States) greets visitors upon their entrance to the West Wing. Here, in the classically appointed reception area, guests wait until they are called into scheduled meetings with White House staffers – or even the President. I created a special bouquet for ROTUS's desk 2 times each week. Surrounded by flowers, she was inspired to start naming the bouquets with such charming monikers as "Midnight Kiss in the Woods," "Sundance Cowboy," "Bahama Mama" and "Tequila Sunrise," based on the color scheme or feeling the flowers evoked. Since Bo (the dog) was a fixture throughout the White House complex and often made daily visits to the East and West Wings, I often incorporated the image of the President's dog in my arrangements, too, tucking a ti or aspidistra leaf cutout into vases and floral displays. The flowers became a source of conversation and a gathering point, providing a daily dose of visual inspiration for West Wing staff and visitors alike. Sometimes, even senior staff and Secret Service agents got involved. The President's Domestic Policy Advisor once named a blue and white bouquet "English Tea Set" because it reminded her of her grandmother's china. ROTUS e-mailed me or stopped by the flower shop whenever she came up with a particularly good name. I loved the idea that the flowers engaged the hard-working staff and gave them a light-hearted moment during the day.

CELEBRITY VISITS

Many White House visitors are surprised to learn that the flower shop resembles any other bustling, busy floral or event studio across the country. Well, almost any other shop. Even though there are the typical stacks of buckets, boxes of flowers, leaves and petals on the floor, a constant flow of bouquets and carts, and staff running in and out – it usually becomes obvious fairly quickly that it's not just any other place. And at no time does this hit home more explicitly than when celebrities pop in, usually without notice or advance warning. It wasn't uncommon for luminaries from the artistic, political, athletic, literary and musical worlds, including famous pop icons to walk in, escorted by White House staffers for an impromptu tour of our flower shop operations: "Hi Laura, this is my friend J.K." (as in Harry Potter author Rowling), "Annie" (pop icon Lennox), "Dierks" (country star Bentley), "Ariana" (pop princess Grande), "Carrie" (Grammy winner Underwood), and on and on.

Hollywood celebrities, famous singers and cultural icons were regular fixtures at the White House, whether it was to participate in one of the Obama Administration's policy initiatives, perform in the White House concert series or attend an official event. One time domestic diva Martha Stewart and her entourage came in while we were working on hand-made holiday containers. "Get a picture of those," she motioned to her assistant, as he snapped away. In general, as White House staffers, our protocol was to maintain a low-key focus on our work to give the celebrity space and respect their privacy during the private tour. But a bold flower shop staffer couldn't resist once she was in Martha Stewart's presence and requested a selfie with the billionaire icon of DIY, which Martha graciously obliged. The flower shop became a regular stop on the VIP "behind-the-scenes" White House tour. Most of the celebrities were friendly and engaging, asking questions about the White House flowers, recounting their own preferences. Television host and cookbook author Rachel Ray, for example, was bubbly and effervescent, telling me about the brightly-colored flowers she likes to keep in her kitchen. Lyle Lovett, singer, song-writer (and actress Julia Roberts' ex-husband) said how much he loves flowers and mentioned the name of his Los Angeles-based florist, urging me to look her up as a potential collaborator. Iconic singer James Taylor made a big impression on me. Gracious and soft-spoken, he told us about his mother's love of flowers and gardening. He said how much she would have loved seeing the flowers and meeting us. He took a picture with me in the cooler and then, to my surprise and delight, gave me a copy of his new CD of Christmas music. Other celebrities quietly slipped in incognito, like academy-award winning actor Leonardo DiCaprio, who wore a visor to cover his face and stood behind his very tall model girlfriend.

One of the more memorable celebrity visits was when superstar performer Justin Timberlake stopped by the flower shop. For that visit in 2013, we received a two minute advance warning, just enough time for me to brief volunteers and remind staff of proper behavior for meeting celebrity visitors. It didn't matter. When JT entered the room, my team (primarily women) gasped so loudly in unison that it literally sucked the air out of the room. There were other people with him, but no one noticed or paid any attention to them. For a moment, we were all speechless and star-struck at being in such close proximity to the multi-talented artist. Obviously, the singer and actor is used to the effect he has on fans. Without missing a beat, he smiled and shook everyone's hand, repeated our names, made some clever commentary about the flowers, and went into the cooler to check out the bouquets that would be used that evening for his performance at the White House "Memphis Soul" event. He was delightful and charming on the VIP tour – and then delivered an epic version of Otis Redding's classic "Sittin' on the Dock of the Bay" later that evening.

OPRAH WINFREY & GAYLE KING.

Oprah Winfrey is a frequent visitor to the Obama White House. For milestone occasions like the President and First Lady's birthdays, special concerts or movie screenings, Oprah usually makes the A-list cut. But she is also a White House regular during quieter times, often accompanied by her BFF Gayle King. A few years ago, they arrived for a casual dinner in the private residence with the President and First Lady. On these occasions, flowers always played a role. I was called on to create flowers for the table, the private residence, and the Truman Balcony, which would serve as a venue for cocktails. As a special treat for her friends, Mrs. Obama also asked me to make little gift bouquets – garden-style arrangement that she would present to Oprah and Gayle as they departed the White House. It was always a pleasure to make these hand-bouquets that I knew would create such happiness for the recipients. I fashioned delicate spring-themed bouquets made of hellebores, roses, jasmine and ferns, finished off with decorated stems, colorful ribbons and a special gift tag made by the White House calligrapher. I kept these flowers in the flower shop cooler until midway through the evening. Then I discreetly made my way up the back elevator to hand off the finished bouquets to the butlers. They placed them on a small vermeil tray that would be brought out at the end of the evening. Later, I heard Oprah's reaction to the flowers from the staff who were there. Oprah and Gayle were apparently leaving the White House late that night, escorted down from the residence and out to their awaiting car at the South Portico entrance. Their flowers were somehow still on the second floor. "Where are our bouquets,?" they both asked, adding, laughing, "we want our flowers!," as an aide scurried quickly to retrieve them.

VICE PRESIDENT BIDEN.

Every year, the Vice President places a special order for anniversary flowers for his wife, Dr. Jill Biden. It is always the same order – a simple bouquet of yellow roses – her favorite flower and personally symbolic to the couple – with one rose symbolizing each year of their marriage. Once I received the call, I prepared and wrapped the roses, getting them ready to go. Sometimes, his staff would ask us to deliver the bouquet to his office, other times, they would race over to the flower shop, grab the bouquet, and place it in the motorcade or Marine One so that the VP would have the flowers in hand wherever his busy official schedule took him. The Vice President is well-known for being gregarious and friendly. One time after our special delivery, he asked his assistant to get our flower shop on the line. We were all out of the office at a meeting, setting up for an event. A flower shop volunteer was the only one there – she took the Vice President's call. "Hello there, what's your name?" he asked in his inimitable way. Carol, the volunteer, was practically speechless when she realized who was on the phone but somehow managed to mumble her name. "Well, Carol, I want you to know the flowers are just great. And you guys are great – you always make me look good." With a "keep up the great work" – he was off the phone and on his way.

126

DR. BIDEN'S GARDEN.

A few years ago in early spring, Dr. Biden asked me to help her with her balcony garden on the 2nd floor of the Old Executive Office Building overlooking the White House. In good weather, she used the balcony as a meeting space or as a quiet space to write and work. She wanted the plantings to look like summer bouquets. Dr. B., as she is affectionately called by staff, is well-known for her kind and thoughtful demeanor. Although gardens aren't really my area of expertise, I wanted to help with her request – and I knew exactly whom to call. One of my flower shop volunteers owns a local nursery and creates beautiful planter gardens for clients. She was excited to volunteer for this special project, and created a beautiful plan for Dr. B.'s pots and planters, which were barren from the harsh winter. With the help of a team of volunteers who were inspired by the gardening challenge, we spent a weekend transforming an empty collection of planters into a colorful and inviting space. Dr. Biden was appreciative of our efforts and her balcony garden became the envy of others in the White House complex. It may have been "mission creep" of my flower-arranging job – but we welcomed the challenge in the spirit of floral diplomacy.

A BRIEF HIATUS.

During my six years of service, I provided flowers day in and day out, with one notable exception: the rancorous budget debates of 2013 when the showdown between the Republican-controlled Congress and the President came to a head and the government shut down. During the shutdown, there were a few people on staff at the White House, a chef, butler, housekeeper and engineers, who were deemed "essential" and would keep working throughout the shutdown. Like curators and middle managers, florists were not deemed to be an "essential" government service. The day of the shutdown we had four hours to shut down our operations, retrieve flowers and vases from throughout the White House complex, clean out the cooler – and basically prepare for an unexpected hiatus when holiday preparations were usually in full swing. We had to turn in our Blackberry devices and could not perform any work during this period. The day of the shutdown, we worked quickly to complete our tasks before the 4 hours was up. When we arrived at the office of the National Security Advisor, who was behind closed doors in a meeting, a staff member earnestly explained: the Ambassador prefers to keep her flowers as long as possible. He said that they would take responsibility for watering them. We conceded, knowing that the flowers would expire long before the government shutdown was over – which turned out to be a long 2 ½ weeks.

IN SUM.

Overall, I worked on close to 2,000 events, everything from small and intimate private parties to large-scale official events, including state dinners. In addition, over 6 years, I created literally tens of thousands of bouquets for the public and private portions of the White House floral portfolio. Stamina and steely resolve are essential components of floral diplomacy.

SUPER BOWL PARTIES.

The Super Bowl is arguably the biggest annual sporting event in the U.S. Over the years, the President and First Lady hosted private viewing parties for the Super Bowl, a party for close friends and family members with big screen televisions and a fun menu of drinks and snacks. During the pre-game show, the President usually gave a network interview, televised live from the Blue Room. Then he would join his guests to watch the football game. This was always a chance to have fun with the decorations. For the Super Bowl party in 2010 (that also coincided with 'Snowmageddon' – the epic snowstorm that paralyzed Washington, D.C.), I took inspiration from the First Lady's Let's Move initiative and crafted little bouquets out of vegetables and fruits for the cocktail tables. I had booked a hotel nearby for the week since it was impossible to travel on the roads. The floral supplier was somehow able to deliver flowers to the snowed-in White House and a skeleton crew of staff helped obtain vegetables for the decorative displays. These arrangements, which were covered in green beans, pearl onions, peppers and Brussels sprouts, were designed to convey a subtle, yet clear message about the importance of healthy eating, albeit in an artistic and decorative way. The nod to Let's Move was mostly in the decorations, though, since the menu included the typical (not-so-healthy) Super Bowl fare of chips, burgers, and buffalo wings. I still wonder how the guests attended the party that evening given the snow-bound state of affairs.

The following year, when the Pittsburgh Steelers played the Green Bay Packers, we took the opposite approach. The linens for the East Room party represented the team colors, divided exactly half and half so as not to reveal a Presidential favorite. Instead of creating designs out of fruits and vegetables, however, we used snack items that would typically be found at a Super Bowl party – creating containers out of chips and gold fish, Cheetos and pretzels and filling them with flowers in the team colors. For the bar, we made two 'footballs' out of beef jerky and pussy willows, which looked remarkably like the real thing. In fact, we heard rumors that later that night (and probably after more than a few beers were consumed), the footballs left their position on the bar and were passed around on the state floor, a report that was neither confirmed nor denied by attendees. If it were indeed the case, however, what an interesting idea – that the decorations themselves inspired some impromptu 'Let's Move' activity. In this case, by using not-so-healthy snack choices in the décor, we focused attention on Let's Move by taking the opposite tack.

In 2014, my favorite team, the Seattle Seahawks, was playing in the Super Bowl against the New England Patriots. For a small Super Bowl party that the President and First Lady hosted in the private residence, we created floral décor that represented the colors of each team. The Seahawks' team colors are blue and green while the Patriots' colors are red, white and blue. The colors were carried out in the ribbon-wrapped vases and in the floral choices. The calligraphers made team logos to match that we used as decorative additions. We placed the flowers throughout the private residence, including a cheering section for both Seahawk and Patriot fans. Since the President typically remains neutral in his team preferences (except for his hometown Chicago teams), the decorations were made exactly half and half to maintain neutrality. Well, maybe there were a couple of extra Seattle designs in the mix. Unfortunately, the Seahawks lost that game in a heart-breaking last second botched goal line play. But we had a good time creating floral diplomacy with a Super Bowl motif.

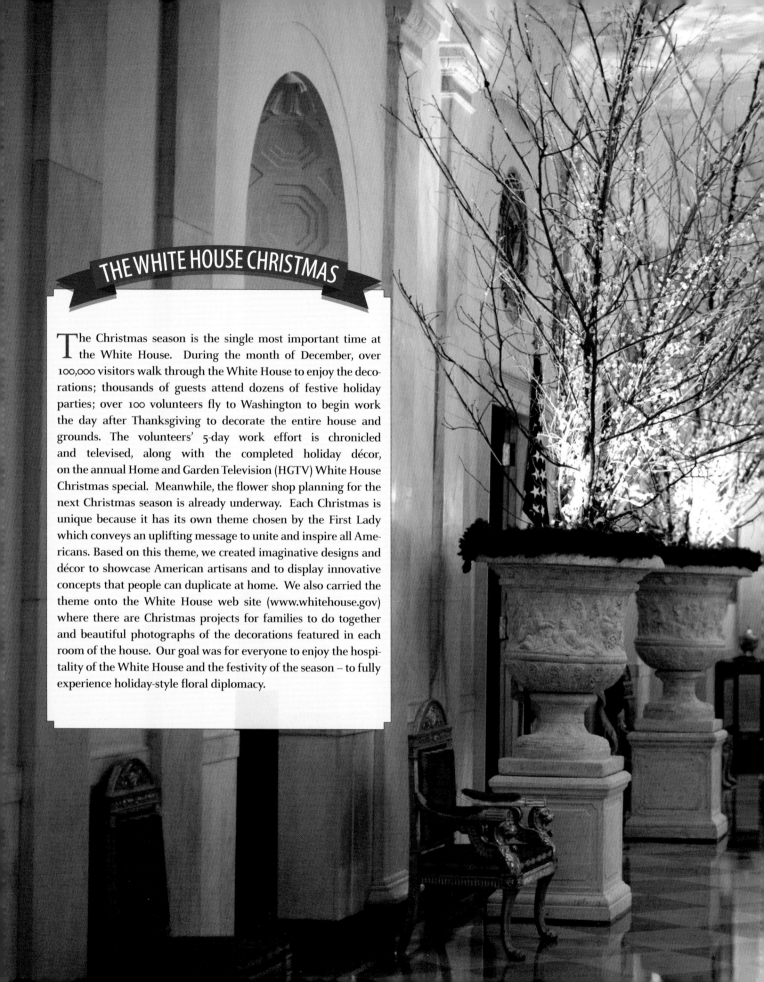

THE WHITE HOUSE CHRISTMAS

The Christmas season is the single most important time at the White House. During the month of December, over 100,000 visitors walk through the White House to enjoy the decorations; thousands of guests attend dozens of festive holiday parties; over 100 volunteers fly to Washington to begin work the day after Thanksgiving to decorate the entire house and grounds. The volunteers' 5-day work effort is chronicled and televised, along with the completed holiday décor, on the annual Home and Garden Television (HGTV) White House Christmas special. Meanwhile, the flower shop planning for the next Christmas season is already underway. Each Christmas is unique because it has its own theme chosen by the First Lady which conveys an uplifting message to unite and inspire all Americans. Based on this theme, we created imaginative designs and décor to showcase American artisans and to display innovative concepts that people can duplicate at home. We also carried the theme onto the White House web site (www.whitehouse.gov) where there are Christmas projects for families to do together and beautiful photographs of the decorations featured in each room of the house. Our goal was for everyone to enjoy the hospitality of the White House and the festivity of the season – to fully experience holiday-style floral diplomacy.

TIME-HONORED TRADITIONS.

Each year throughout December, the White House holiday season is a celebration of the spirit of optimism, hopefulness and imagination that embodies the Christmas season – a magical time of year when all dreams seem possible and families revel in cherished memories and time-honored traditions. Since 1889, when Benjamin Harrison brought the first Christmas tree into the White House Yellow Oval Room, First Families have put their personal stamp on the nation's holiday home and created private memories of celebrating the season. Each year, the White House becomes a magical winter wonderland of over 50 lavishly decorated holiday trees, colorful ornaments, miles of cedar and pine garlands, and twinkling lights, an incredible and awe-inspiring sight. For my team of designers and volunteers, it was a chance to create something new and inspirational for over 100,000 visitors to see in person on White House holiday tours and millions more to see in the Home and Garden Television's (HGTV) annual holiday special. With the advent of Pinterest, Google+ hangouts, Twitter, Facebook and Instagram, it became possible to share beautiful White House décor with an audience world-wide.

Without a doubt, the most exciting and complex project of the year was the planning process that goes into creating the White House Christmas displays. It was also my favorite challenge. The elaborate planning and brainstorming starts a year in advance involving the selection of a theme and key elements of the décor in collaboration with the First Lady, development of sketches and prototypes, the selection of the Blue Room tree, and the launch of intricate design projects that require the help of hundreds of volunteers. The ambition and scale of these projects make them interesting and noteworthy. Among the inspiring and innovative designs we created in recent years are a ribbon and pipe cleaner archway featuring thousands of pieces of pipe cleaners arranged in a complex latticework motif; the illusion cube column covers made from tens of thousands of berries, folded leaves and individual gold leaf pine cone scales; the doorway frame made of 1,000 gilded oak leaf rosettes; the Red Room sugar flower vases; oversized wreaths made out of lacquered fruits and vegetables; and the ever-popular replicas of the Presidential dogs Bo and Sunny made out of 40,000 pipe cleaners, miles of looped ribbon, licorice and marshmallows, buttons, and even trash bags. Once the initial themes, sub-themes and room by room plans were in place, I developed prototypes and action plans. It was a year-round effort.

To spark creative inspiration, I often walked around the state and ground floors during the Christmas holiday season, making notes for ideas and décor for the following year. It was much easier to visualize Christmas during the actual season than in July or August when the temperatures soared into the high 90s and there was a dearth of holiday greenery, if not holiday cheer. Whenever I traveled, I was always on the lookout for patterns and motifs to incorporate in holiday designs: a trellis pattern from Versailles, a geometric tile motif from Florence, a floral plaster motif from Paris. I kept a notebook of ideas and then worked with volunteer artists and architects to create sketches and renderings of specific designs. My use of technology definitely evolved and improved during my tenure. My first two planning ventures at the White House involved taping sample ornaments to recycled cardboard flower boxes along with ribbons, fabrics, and greenery as concepts to present to the First Lady and her staff – a decidedly low-tech approach. Meanwhile, in the outside world, I saw how Pinterest and design blogs were creating digital inspiration boards that took design presentations to the next level. It required special computer technology and graphics programs that were not available to me at the White House given budget constraints. So I found talented volunteers, adept at taking my ideas for colors, images and design elements and translating them into these digital presentations, to create them. The "inspiration boards" were an essential part of my process for articulating design proposals for Christmas, State Dinners, and other important official events.

SIMPLE GIFTS.

The most memorable White House holiday season was 2010, the year the First Lady chose "Simple Gifts" as the holiday theme. The idea for the theme came to me on an evening walk in the middle of winter almost a year before. I challenged myself to come up with a theme that would exemplify the First Lady's inclusive spirit and positive tone, set an inspirational message, provide opportunities for creative décor and sub-themes, and tell a story room by room. During the décor preview with the First Lady, where I presented color schemes and projects for each space, we sat down at the large table in her office. The chefs brought in a selection of holiday cookies and the butlers poured a sparkly cranberry drink in champagne glasses which they served to the handful of staff in the room. It was a casual and light-hearted meeting with Mrs. Obama and her team. She said that she wanted the décor to represent each Obama family member, including the President, First Lady, Malia, Sasha, Grandmother and First Family dog Bo.

The First Lady loved the theme of "Simple Gifts" – everything from the overarching message to the ideas for translating the meaning of simple gifts of the holidays into specific décor for each White House room: the gift of music, the gift of family traditions, the gift of nature, the gift of celebrations, etc. We attempted some of our most ambitious work that year which is still featured on design blogs as a "Spectacular White House Christmas." To carry out the expansive list of handmade projects – over 60 in all – I created a spreadsheet that chronicled the steps and resources required to execute all of the complex designs. I brought in teams of local volunteers to assist the detailed craft projects – 1,000 gilded oak leaf rosettes, thousands of handmade ribbon poinsettias made from re-purposed ribbon, 40,000 black and white pipe cleaners to make the replica of First Family dog Bo. We started creating these elements in the summer. Some of the innovations included creating a holiday table setting featuring White House china in the China Room and commissioning a local iron worker to fashion three double arches that spanned the concave ceilings of the Lower Cross Hall that can be re-used every year. In 2010, the arches were covered in natural greenery and silk holiday ribbon in keeping with the "Simple Gifts" theme. My planning process involved creating a room-by-room design template that we followed in our holiday preparations year after year.

SPECIAL PROJECTS.

Some projects stand out for their sheer audacity and ambition. The "illusion cube column covers" that was first displayed during the White House holidays 2012 was that kind of project. I was inspired to create something beautiful in the East Entrance – a space that was often overlooked in previous holiday décor. My idea was to create column covers that would fit over the four sandstone columns on either side of the East Entrance foyer. These would be made from simple plywood sheets – a 3-sided form cut to fit over the columns. The pattern – a festive and classical illusion cube motif – 3D cubes made of red berries, folded green leaves and gold pine cone scales – is an elegant pattern that also has a modern, geometric feel. It was an intense project: thousands and thousands of individual pieces of material were painstakingly prepared, organized and then glued onto the carefully drawn and measured pieces. We launched the project the summer before the holidays. One special volunteer served as the project lead. She came in every day for nearly 6 months to work on this one project. Another volunteer who is an architect measured the cube design using her arm as a protractor – creating a perfectly rendered pattern of connecting diagonal lines that was traced onto the plywood surface. As we approached the deadline for installation, additional volunteers worked with me day and night to complete the project. The decorative column covers were installed as free-standing pieces so as not to damage the wood or architectural features. They looked beautiful in the space. That year, an observant volunteer noted that the illusion cube motif appears elsewhere in the White House – on the early 19th century marble-topped table in the Red Room designed by French-American cabinetmaker Charles Honore Lannuier – one of the most important and valuable pieces in the White House collection. It was a serendipitous coincidence of holiday-style floral diplomacy.

The best part about decorating the White House for Christmas was knowing the joy it brought to the thousands of visitors who came there throughout the season, especially the children who experienced the special decorations that we created just for them, such as the Bo and Sunny topiaries. It was that sense of wonder and excitement that made the months of planning and hard work all worthwhile. For me, personally, I loved the fact that people were inspired to try some of our ideas and decorations at home. Through social media channels, we shared White House designs and inspiration, including step by step instructions and tutorials, with a wide audience, opening up the White House to all Americans and people around the world. In addition to the Bo topiary and Bo-bot displays, we incorporated the family dogs in several different holiday designs.

BO-FLAKES.

One year at a family holiday gathering at my sister's house in Seattle, I noticed the place cards at the beautifully appointed table. They were little white wedges with our names cut into them. When we opened them up, they became snowflakes with our individual names forming distinctive and charming patterns in the snowflake form. They were fabulous. I found out that they were the handiwork of my 16-year-old niece. I took my place card snowflake back to the White House and taped it to the window behind my computer. When we started the annual holiday planning process, I had an idea. What if we took the concept – the hand-made, patterned snowflakes that were at our holiday table and turned them into snowflakes with a White House-specific theme: snow-flakes with a "Bo" (First Family dog) motif? I went back to my niece with the challenge: could she craft 5 or 6 different designs that we could use as part of the White House Christmas décor? Without missing a beat, she called the Bo-themed snowflake project "Bo-flakes." And then she responded with a collection that blew everyone away. I had them duplicated and die-cut on an adhesive backing that we placed on lucite discs. These were hung on a small tree in the Booksellers area as a backdrop to the ribbon-covered Bo replica. We also created enough Bo-flakes to use as the children's craft project for the holiday press preview;

kids chose a Bo-flake design and then added festive ribbons. The Bo-flakes captured the imagination of visitors and the press alike. They were one of the highlights of the season. That year, I invited my sister and niece to join me at the holiday staff party where we had our photo taken with the President and First Lady. When I introduced the President to my niece, Erica, and told him that she was the mastermind behind the popular Bo-flake designs, he grinned broadly, saying "Great job with the Bo-flakes, Erica!" We all smiled at the sound of President Obama saying "Bo-flake."

BO & SUNNY HOUNDSTOOTH MOTIF.

In 2014, I again went back to my talented family for volunteer support. In a late night e-mail, I challenged my sister Bonnie, a graphic artist, with an idea. My concept was a pattern or motif that we could use in various applications throughout the White House holiday décor. "I want to create a bold, graphic pattern with a Bo and Sunny (the new family dog) motif," I said, "what do you think?" Within a couple of hours, Bonnie sent me a prototype design that was pure genius – she had created a classic black and white "houndstooth" pattern – with Bo and Sunny incorporated into the design. After refining the design, we digitized the pattern and turned it into special wrapping paper that was widely used in the décor. It also became a popular interactive part of the White House holidays that people could download from the White House web site. The houndstooth paper was a big hit: some staffers even suggested that we turn it into ties or pants that could be sold at the White House gift shop.

"BO-TALES."

Another popular dog-themed project was the "Bo-tale" ornaments we created for display throughout the White House. These designs, featuring Bo and Sunny in various holiday vignettes – singing holiday carols, decorating a Christmas tree, baking cookies, sledding, wrapping presents, making snow angels, creating snowflakes, and other charming scenes. The ornaments were hand-colored and transferred onto recycled paper ornaments. In the holiday tour book, the 12 Bo and Sunny themed ornaments became a game for children: a clue for finding the ornament was pictured in the book; the children then looked for the corresponding ornament in each room. In addition, for the press preview craft project with children, we created little notebooks that featured all of the vignettes and invited children to create and color their own holiday tale.

Other favorite projects included architectural – inspired decorations for the East Colonnade. In 2012 , we covered an existing iron frame in plywood, painted it red and then covered it in red ribbon. My idea was to create a garden trellis design using green pipe cleaners applied in an intricate pattern. After taking a digital image of the design, we transferred it by tracing the pattern with charcoal pencil on to the ribbon. The key to this kind of design is absolute precision starting at the top and then working from the middle to the outside edges, maintaining the pattern and overall visual balance. We took a very organized approach: I asked the carpenters to create small blocks of wood that would serve as patterns for the pipe cleaner pieces. The pattern involved creating two shapes – rectangles and squares – and two connecting pieces of different lengths. Volunteers folded and cut all of the elements and placed them in separate baskets. This project required thousands of pieces of pipe cleaner to create the trellis arch.

Another year, we used dried hydrangea to create a burgundy and green chevron-patterned frame for the same space. Once again, the starting point was precision measuring and drawing of the pattern, which involved marking the alternating green and burgundy stripes and gluing hydrangea florets onto the frame. In 2014, we created new column covers for the East Entrance – a classic diamond pattern motif of boxwood pieces glued over ice blue fabric. The boxwood was enhanced with red winterberries and crystals to evoke an overall festive and wintry effect. We carried out the diamond pattern motif by crafting special containers and pedestals for floral displays. The combination of the ice blue with dark red roses, nandina berries and winter greens complemented the holiday theme and "winter wonderland" décor.

Each year, the White House Christmas was an opportunity to represent the essence of the holiday season: spending time with friends and family, giving thanks and counting blessings, celebrating the joy of children, honoring America's military men and women, and decorating the home with beautiful materials from the winter garden. It was always my hope that the spirit of warmth of generosity, of celebrating what unites all of us during the Christmas holiday season, would be translated into the White House holiday décor – to create an inspirational example of floral diplomacy.

"FLOWER AMBASSADOR"

THE POWER OF FLOWERS

In the aftermath of the tragic terrorist attack in Paris in November 2015, there was one heart-warming and inspiring scene that stood out as an iconic moment. At the Bataclan Theatre, mourners paid tribute to those whose lives were cut short, placing flowers and candles at the scene of the attack, creating an oasis of beauty in a city awash in sorrow and grief. At this makeshift memorial site, a small boy and his father were engaged in a conversation that was caught on camera for the world to hear. "There's bad guys, Daddy; they can shoot us because they're really, really mean." "Yes, they might have guns, but we have flowers," replied the father. "But flowers don't do anything," the boy said. "Of course they do. Look, everyone is putting flowers down. It's to fight the guns," said the father. "For protection?" "Yes." The boy turned to the reporter and said: "The flowers are here to protect us."

The orchard in bloom,
re-born every year again,
we salute its blossoms

Haiku written by European Council President
Emeritus Herman van Rompuy
In honor of the "Flower Ambassador" award presented to
Laura Dowling at Floralien 2016, Ghent, Belgium

As this amazing scene went viral, it captured the imagination of people around the world. In that split second, we saw the face of innocence in an unpredictable and dangerous world, a father's love for his innocent child and his evocative description of flowers taking on symbolic importance as a tool against the war on terror. The flowers that people were placing at this monument symbolized a glimmer of hope, highlighting the power and strength of the human spirit. The attention from the interview with the little boy solidified the resolve of the French people and inspired millions of others throughout the world.

In April 2016, I was honored to participate in Floralien, an international floral fair in Ghent, Belgium, that dates back to the early 19th century. This major event sponsored by the Royal Horticultural Society of Belgium takes place every four years and involves floral artists from around the world creating inspiring installations throughout this medieval town. My exhibit was part of an installation that paid tribute to soldiers who perished in World War I, a memorial garden depicting Flanders field where so many soldiers lost their lives. The organizers asked me to create an installation highlighting the theme of "floral diplomacy." I proposed an inspirational piece to symbolize peace, freedom and democracy. I settled on the idea of creating a floral dome reminiscent of the U.S. Capitol made out of natural materials and finished with a dove of peace. The floral dome stood at the edge of the battlefield as an iconic symbol of liberty, peace and of the promise of hope and renewal. Floralien took place close in time and location to the terrorist attacks on the Brussels airport and, like the placement of bouquets at the Bataclan in Paris, illustrated the healing power of flowers in peoples' minds. It reinforced the universal message of floral diplomacy: that flowers provide hope and comfort in challenging times.

At the White House, flowers bring people together. They are important and expected at both private and public events, creating beauty and providing a "floral framework" for building a conducive environment that encourages collaboration and understanding. Looking forward, there is great potential for expanding on the initial ideas of floral diplomacy we established. For instance, the next administration could expand the White House kitchen garden to incorporate a flower cutting garden, highlighting the importance of locally and organically grown flowers at the White House, sending a powerful message to environmentalists, gardeners and growers – and all Americans. In addition, there is room to strengthen and regularize the relationship between the flower shop, policy staff and communications teams in order to create new opportunities for important messages to resonate. Finally, the next administration could encourage the U.S. State Department to embrace floral diplomacy (like culinary or cultural diplomacy) by promoting international floral installations as a way to enhance diplomatic exchange and understanding.

Floral diplomacy has a voice that resonates globally, evoking feelings and understanding that transcend time, place and circumstances. Like the orchard in bloom referenced in European Council President van Rompuy's haiku or the fruit orchard of my long-ago family farm, flower blossoms are fragile yet strong, reflecting the resiliency of the human spirit. Fleeting yet enduring. Dependable. Beautiful. Eternal.

The concept for this book took root in Ghent, Belgium, in April 2016 with the encouragement of the members of the Board of the Royal Horticultural Society of Belgium and Floralien. Michel Vermaerke, Gudrun Cottenier and others organized the most inspiring display of international floral art that I have ever seen, including a special World War I exhibit that paid tribute to fallen soldiers. In this symbolic space, the concept of using flowers and gardens to convey comfort during difficult times inspired me to create a stylized "floral dome" signifying peace and democracy. Occurring just a short time after the tragic terrorist attack at the Brussels Airport, Floralien's themes of international cooperation and "floral diplomacy" took on increased significance and poignancy. My participation in Floralien helped me put a name to my strategic use of flowers at the White House and created the intellectual framework for the book.

I am extremely grateful for the opportunity to collaborate with StichtingKunstBoek, whose beautiful books on floral art and design have long been a part of my reference library. It's been a pleasure to work with publisher Karel Puype, editor Katrien Van Moerbeke and designer Jan de Coster who have made the process of writing this book such a joy. They worked diligently across time zones to help me tell my personal story of White House floral diplomacy.

So many colleagues in the floral world have supported my passion for design and strategic approach that are represented in this book. I'm especially indebted to former White House Social Secretary Desiree Rogers for her visionary leadership and for taking the bold step to venture outside the norm to launch a merit-based competition for the White House floral position. My deep gratitude extends to the army of staff and volunteers who were equally inspired by my vision of flowers as a strategic tool and worked tirelessly side by side with me for so many years to create beauty at the White House. I am also lucky to have

the support of an extended village of friends and family members who have encouraged me every step of the way, especially Elizabeth Vale, my Garden Club friends and Old Town neighbors, Winifred and John Constable who generously opened their home and garden as a backdrop to many floral creations that are featured in the book, and my family members – including my mom, siblings, cousins, aunts, uncles and in-laws who provided creative insights and moral support. Michele Hatty Fritz created the beautiful calligraphy for the cover.

My husband, Bob Weinhagen, supports all of my creative pursuits, and I am so grateful for his love and encouragement, brilliant insights and dry humor.

Finally, I want to express my deep gratitude to the President and First Lady for giving me the honor and privilege of serving as Chief Floral Designer at the White House and for inspiring me to reach higher in all of my work.

PHOTOGRAPHY CREDITS

As a floral artist, I am keenly aware of the ephemeral nature of flowers and the transient quality of my creations. Flowers and photography go hand in hand. Photography captures the fleeting reality of floral art as well as the special moments that might otherwise go unnoticed, and, in any event, will soon be gone forever. I am grateful to the photographers who provided images for this book including Edward Gehman Kohan of ObamaFoodorama, Georgianna Lane, Kevin Allen, Kate Headley, Phil Yabut, Lynn Sauls, Cory Stajduhar, Getty images, the White House Photo Office and several talented flower shop volunteers. While I was working in the moment, often too busy to stop and reflect on the scene around me, they had the presence of mind to document floral arrangements that tell the story of White House "floral diplomacy."

Laura — Thanks for helping to make the White House so beautiful!

Author
Laura Dowling
www.lauradowling.com

Layout
www.groupvandamme.eu

Published by
Stichting Kunstboek bvba
Legeweg 165
B-8020 Oostkamp
info@stichtingkunstboek.com
www.stichtingkunstboek.com

ISBN 978-90-5856-558-7
D/2016/6407/21
NUR 421

Printed in the EU